W9-AYX-778

Traits of Good Writing

2-3

Written by
Mary Murray

Editor: Carla Hamaguchi
Illustrator: Darcy Tom
Designer: Moonhee Pak
Cover Designer: Barbara Peterson
Art Director: Tom Cochrane
Project Director: Carolea Williams

© 2004 Creative Teaching Press, Inc., Huntington Beach, CA 92649
Reproduction of activities in any manner for use in the classroom and not for commercial sale is permissible.
Reproduction of these materials for an entire school or for a school system is strictly prohibited.

Table of Contents

Introduction

Each book in the *Power Practice*™ series contains dozens of ready-to-use activity pages to provide students with skill practice. Use the fun activities to supplement and enhance what you are already teaching in your classroom. Give an activity page to students as independent class work, or send the pages home as homework to reinforce skills taught in class. An answer key is provided for quick reference.

The activity pages in *Traits of Good Writing 2–3* provide an ideal way to enhance students' writing skills. The book features activities that target six important traits of writing: Ideas and Content, Organization, Voice, Word Choice, Sentence Fluency, and Conventions. These fun and challenging activities give students many opportunities to practice each writing skill in a meaningful way.

As students learn to recognize the traits of good writing, they will brainstorm and develop topics, develop and organize their thoughts and ideas, and then put their writing skills into practice. Students will gain confidence in their writing ability as they enhance grammar and usage skills and gain an awareness of how word choice and sentence development influences their writing. As your young authors establish a style and voice of their own, they will be well on their way to becoming successful and competent writers.

Use these ready-to-go activities to "recharge" skill review and give students the power to succeed!

What Do You Know?

Brainstorming Topics

A good writer will write about what he or she knows. Look at the topics. Brainstorm ideas for each topic. Write your ideas in the bubble.

school

friends

family

foods

Traits of Good Writing • 2–3 © 2004 Creative Teaching Press

Picture Perfect

Gathering Ideas

You can get ideas for writing by looking at pictures. Look at each picture. Then write a sentence that describes a story based on the picture.

_____

_____

_____

_____

_____

_____

_____

_____

_____

_____

_____

_____

Traits of Good Writing • 2–3 © 2004 Creative Teaching Press

Experiences

Brainstorming Ideas

Experiences give you ideas for writing. What interesting experiences have you had? Maybe you have caught tadpoles, rode a city bus, or built a robot. Look at each picture. Write a title for it.

_____

_____

_____

_____

_____

_____

_____

_____

_____

_____

_____

_____

Name _____

Outdoor Fun

Brainstorming Content

You are going to write about having fun outdoors. Write an idea in each square.

 Now narrow it down. Color in the squares of the three ideas that would be easiest for you to write about. Then, write everything you know about one of those topics.

Traits of Good Writing • 2–3 © 2004 Creative Teaching Press

It's Time to Write

Writing Prompts

A writing prompt can help you think of ideas to write about.
Writing that shares information or explains something is called **expository** writing.
Writing that tells a story is called **narrative** writing.

Read each writing prompt. Shade in the circle next to the letter **E** if it's an expository writing prompt. Shade in the circle next to the letter **N** if it's a narrative writing prompt.

1 Explain how to make a root beer float.	**2** Write about a spaceship that landed in your backyard.	**3** Tell how to get to your house from school.
E ○ N ○	E ○ N ○	E ○ N ○
4 Write a letter to your parents explaining why you're old enough to sleep over at a friend's house.	**5** Tell what happened on your last family vacation.	**6** Explain the likenesses and differences between soccer and kickball.
E ○ N ○	E ○ N ○	E ○ N ○
7 Tell about a funny experience that you and a friend had together.	**8** Gather information about giraffes and write what you learn.	**9** Tell about a girl who loves to ride horses.
E ○ N ○	E ○ N ○	E ○ N ○

 Use the writing prompt that you like best to write an expository piece or a narrative story.

Let's Explore

Gathering Information

> Exploring, investigating, and gathering information are important skills to use when writing. Even if you know a lot about a subject, you can still find out more.

Read each writing topic. Where could you find information about it? Cross out the letter of the item that you would **not** use to gather information.

1 Topic: Abraham Lincoln

   a. check the dictionary
   b. read the encyclopedia
   c. go to the book store
   d. look on the Internet

2 Topic: apples

   a. visit an apple orchard
   b. look at maps
   c. taste different apples
   d. read the encyclopedia

3 Topic: basketball

   a. read magazines
   b. check an atlas
   c. go to a basketball game
   d. talk to basketball players

4 Topic: computers

   a. read magazines
   b. go to an electronics store
   c. go to a restaurant
   d. ask a neighbor who
       programs computers

5 Topic: dogs

   a. visit a kennel
   b. ask a neighbor who has
       a dog
   c. visit an aquarium
   d. go to the library

6 Topic: my school

   a. talk to a teacher
   b. visit the principal's office
   c. read the school newspaper
   d. read the encyclopedia

Traits of Good Writing • 2-3 © 2004 Creative Teaching Press

Project Pet

Categorizing Details

Organizing ideas and details before you begin writing is important. Look at the ideas and details in the word box. Write each idea and detail in the graphic organizer.

> carrots   eats   hold her   brush her coat
> grass   build a maze for her   feed 2 times a day   oranges
> bathe once a week   clean her cage   apples   sleeps   plays
> squeaks when I get home   clip her nails   water

Daily Activities	**What She Eats/Drinks**

Leah the guinea pig

Fun Things to Do with Leah	**How to Care for Leah**

Traits of Good Writing • 2–3 © 2004 Creative Teaching Press

Name _____

My City

Organizing Details

Help this student organize the information about her city. Write each piece of information from the box under the correct heading.

Wisconsin River
Lunch Bucket Café
Whistle Stop Sandwich Shop
Historical Museum
Annual City Garage Sale
Nature Days

Lake Marion
Gordon's Diner
Crystal Lake
The Cheese Factory
July Fourth Celebration

Indian Lake State Park
Taco City
Sky High Apple Orchard
Art Gallery
Arts and Crafts Festival

Mazomanie, Wisconsin

Nature and Parks

_____

_____

_____

_____

Restaurants

_____

_____

_____

Fun Places to Visit

_____

_____

_____

Annual Events and Activities

_____

_____

_____

 Fold a separate sheet of paper twice to make a three-fold brochure. Write about your city inside the brochure. Draw pictures of places to see and things to do.

Traits of Good Writing • 2–3 © 2004 Creative Teaching Press

Name _____

Ideas and More

Choosing Topics and Adding Details

Write one topic for each heading. Then write three details (things you know) about each topic.

Food: [   ]

_____

_____

_____

Animals: [   ]

_____

_____

_____

Toys: [   ]

_____

_____

_____

Traits of Good Writing • 2-3 © 2004 Creative Teaching Press

A Humorous Story

Organizing a Narrative

Help organize this narrative. Write each term next to the matching part of the narrative.

conclusion	second event	characters	third event
setting	first event	problem	most important moment

1 Paul and I _____

2 At Paul's house, we had to help with his little sister's birthday party _____

3 We wanted our day to be more exciting and fun. _____

4 First, we help the three-year-olds play games. _____

5 Then, we help serve cake and ice cream. _____

6 Finally, we get to play basketball in the driveway and Paul makes me laugh. _____

7 Paul hops on his sister's tricycle and coasts down the hill. He crashes at the bottom of the hill and lands in a big puddle of water. We laugh hard. _____

8 All the little girls laugh, too. Paul ended up being the entertainment. _____

Traits of Good Writing • 2–3 © 2004 Creative Teaching Press

Details

Adding Details

It's important to add details when writing about a specific topic. The details should be interesting, important, and informative to the reader. Don't write details the reader already knows.

Read the two paragraphs. Which one features interesting, important, and informative details?

DAILY NEWS

Last night there was a thunderstorm. It rained a lot. It thundered a lot. The thunderstorm lasted a long time. Many branches fell because of the wind.

A huge thunderstorm blew through Blue Mounds around nine o'clock last night. Rain poured down for more than five hours. By morning a total of three inches of rain had saturated the ground. There were wind gusts up to 40 miles per hour, causing several trees to fall. The power was out for two hours due to down power lines. The three-inch downpour broke a 1989 record for rainfall, when two and a half inches of rain fell in one day.

Read the sentence about a snowstorm. What details could you add to it? Write your ideas below.

Yesterday we had a blizzard in our city.

_____

_____

_____

_____

A Trip to the Library

Details

Color in the books that have a detail for a story about a trip to the library. Remember to include details that are important and interesting and that share information. Do not include details the reader already knows.

My mom and I rode our bikes to the library.

The librarian said, "It's important to read a lot."

Mom helped me find books I like.

I can't wait for supper because we're having pizza.

I found two books to help me with my report on iguanas.

Mom and I sat in the rockers and read.

The librarian helped us check out our books.

My uncle works in a pet store.

Traits of Good Writing • 2–3 © 2004 Creative Teaching Press

Start a Story

Story Starters

A "story starter" helps you get an idea for writing. Read each story starter. Choose the one that you like best. Write it on the first line. Then write the rest of the story. After you finish the story, write a title at the top.

It was the best birthday surprise I ever had.

I never had so much fun on a rainy day.

This was going to be the best Saturday our family ever spent together.

There's nothing better than getting a brand-new pet.

Title

_____

_____

_____

_____

_____

_____

_____

_____

Name _____

For the Birds

Compare and Contrast

It's important to organize ideas and information when comparing and contrasting two things. You can organize information by how things are alike and how they are different using a Venn diagram. The parts that overlap show you ways in which the two birds are alike.

Read the information on the Venn diagram. Then answer the questions.

Flamingo **Ostrich**

Grows to 5 feet tall

Has a very flexible neck

Its bill bends downward

Lays eggs in the mud

Have long necks

Have long legs

Lay eggs

Have feathers

Have wings

Cannot fly

Runs fast; up to 40 mph

Grows to 8 feet tall

Weighs up to 300 pounds

Lays eggs in sand

1 Write 2 ways that the flamingo and ostrich are the same.

_____

_____

2 Write 2 ways that the birds are different.

_____

_____

Traits of Good Writing • 2-3 © 2004 Creative Teaching Press

A Friendly Letter

Letter Writing

Complete the crossword puzzle using the labels for the parts of a friendly letter.

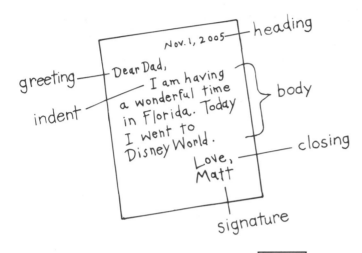

Across
2. This part of the letter shares information. It's what you have to say.
3. The date and/or your address
4. When you sign your name, it's called your _____.

Down
1. With love; Sincerely; Your friend
5. Do this to each paragraph in the body of a letter.
6. This part of the letter says "hello." It usually begins with "Dear."

 Write a letter to a friend or family member. Be sure to include all parts of the letter.

Name _____

Bake a Pizza

Sequencing Instructions

These instructions for baking a pizza are out of order. What should happen first? Number the boxes from one to six to sequence the directions in the right order.

Place the pizza in the oven.

Unwrap the pizza.

Cut it into slices and enjoy.

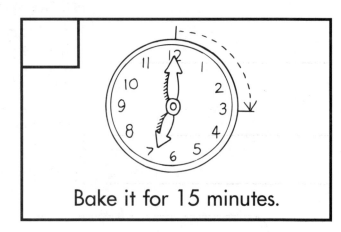

Bake it for 15 minutes.

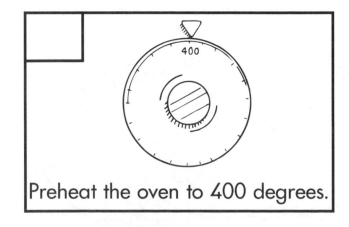

Preheat the oven to 400 degrees.

Remove the pizza from the oven.

Traits of Good Writing • 2–3 © 2004 Creative Teaching Press

Name _____

Fishbowl

Transitions

Sequence the instructions for cleaning a fishbowl. Write the correct word in front of each sentence so that the sentences are clearly in order and easy to understand.

First	Then	After that
Second	Finally	Next

_____ scoop out the fish and put them in a different container of water.

_____ carefully dump out the dirty water. Don't let the pebbles fall into the drain.

_____ wash and scrub the sides of the bowl and the rocks with soapy water.

_____ rinse the bowl several times until no more soap bubbles appear.

_____ add fresh water to the bowl.

_____ put the fish back into the clean bowl.

Traits of Good Writing • 2–3 © 2004 Creative Teaching Press

Make Your Bed

Writing Instructions

Help organize the instructions for making a bed. Write these three instructions in the correct order below.

- Arrange your stuffed animals on top of the bed.

- Pull up the blanket so that it covers the sheet.

- Place the pillow at the top and center of the bed.

1) Remove from the bed all the stuffed animals that you have slept with.

2) _____

3) Pull up the sheet so that it covers the pillow.

4) _____

5) Pull the comforter up and over everything.

6) _____

7) Put your pajamas away and have a great day.

On another sheet of paper write directions for making an ice-cream sundae. Be sure your writing is clear and that the steps are in order.

Traits of Good Writing • 2–3 © 2004 Creative Teaching Press

Name _____

What's the Topic?

Topic Sentences

A topic sentence is the first sentence in the paragraph and tells what the paragraph is about. Read each paragraph. Circle the topic sentence and write the topic on the line.

1 Topic _____

> Puppies make wonderful pets. Puppies like to play. They're small enough to carry in your arms. It's fun to take a puppy on a walk. I wish puppies would stay small forever.

2 Topic _____

> Fishing is a great sport for kids and adults. Learning which bait attracts the best fish is important. It's fun to bait your own hook. Fishing is relaxing, but it also takes patience. It's great to be outdoors on a summer day. It's best if you can fish from a boat, but it's also great to fish from shore. Everyone who tries fishing will probably enjoy it.

3 Topic _____

> School is great! You get to be with your friends all day. You learn a lot about different subjects. The teachers are nice, and recess is fun. School is the perfect place to spend the day.

4 Topic _____

> My grandpa is a great guy. He always jokes around with me and makes me laugh. I get to eat anything I want when I'm at his house. Grandpa tells me interesting stories about when he was young. I'm glad I get to see my grandpa each week.

Traits of Good Writing • 2-3 © 2004 Creative Teaching Press

Cold Lunch Is Cool

Details and the Main Idea

Color in the children who are sharing a detail that supports the main idea.

Main Idea: | I'd rather eat a cold lunch from home than a hot lunch at school.

You don't have to wait in a long line to get your lunch.

Mr. Dupee is a great gym teacher.

You don't have to bring money to the office each week.

I have a dentist appointment on Friday.

You don't have to wonder about what's for lunch and worry that you might not like it.

You can ask your mom to pack your favorite foods.

You can have a fun lunch box.

My mom made my Halloween costume.

Traits of Good Writing • 2–3 © 2004 Creative Teaching Press

Name _____

Kickball

Details

Color in the ball next to the sentence if it contains a detail that is important to the topic of kickball. Cross out the ball if the detail is not important.

- Stretch your legs before game time.
- Wear good tennis shoes.
- Mom bought me a purple T-shirt.
- Practice running and kicking often.
- Show good sportsmanship.
- We're having hamburgers for supper tonight.
- Grandma is coming to visit this summer.
- Cheer on your team.
- Kick as hard as you can.
- Be ready to catch a fly ball.
- I always watch cartoons before the game.

Write a strong concluding sentence about kickball.

_____

_____

Traits of Good Writing • 2-3 © 2004 Creative Teaching Press

Name _____

My Favorite Drinks

Paragraph Organization

A **paragraph** has three main parts: beginning, middle, and end. A paragraph is always indented.

The beginning is the topic sentence. ⟶
| Hot chocolate is my favorite drink on a cold day. |

The middle is the body, which includes details about the topic. ⟶

| It tastes great. | It warms you up. | It makes you feel good inside and out. |

The end is the closing sentence, which reminds the reader what the paragraph is about. It may restate the topic sentence in a new way. ⟶

| I always choose hot chocolate on a winter day. |

Complete the paragraph web. Add three supporting details about orange juice.

| Orange juice is a great drink anytime of day. |

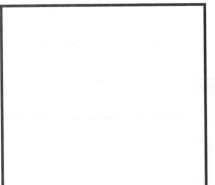 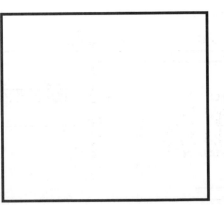

| Orange juice is my favorite beverage. |

Traits of Good Writing • 2–3 © 2004 Creative Teaching Press

Basketball Days

Sequencing a Story

Look at the pictures. Think of a name for the boy and then write a sentence next to each picture to tell a story.

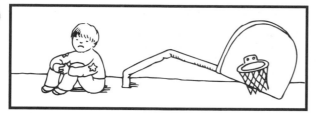

_____
_____
_____

_____

_____
_____
_____

_____

_____
_____
_____

_____

_____
_____
_____

_____

Name _____

Zachary's New Friends

Beginning, Middle, End

> The **beginning** of a story tells who, what, and where. It introduces a problem or conflict. The **middle** of a story tells what happens. The **end** of a story tells how the problem or conflict was resolved.

The parts of this story are out of order. Label each paragraph **beginning, middle,** or **end.** Then reread the story.

When Zachary noticed a parade at the other end of his block, he ran to watch the floats and listen to the band. The kids on one float threw Zachary a T-shirt and invited him to hop on for a ride. They wanted Zachary to play on their baseball team. Zachary quickly hopped on. He was happy to join their team. Zachary goes to practice every day and now he has many new friends.

_____

Zachary tried everything he could think of to meet other children. He set up a lemonade stand in his front yard. He did stunts on his bicycle in the driveway to attract attention. He set up a table at the curb to sell baseball cards. But no children stopped at Zachary's house, no matter what he did.

_____

Zachary and his mother moved into a small white house in a town called Cottage Grove. Zachary wanted to make new friends right away this time. He knew that the first few days after a move were when he felt the loneliest.

_____

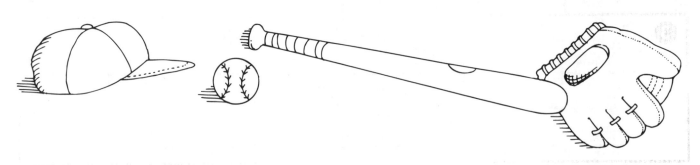

Traits of Good Writing • 2-3 © 2004 Creative Teaching Press

Name _____

My Life

Story Web

Write a story about your life. Think of six important things that have happened in your lifetime. Fill in the web with your ideas. You might want to begin with the most important event—the day you were born. Be sure to keep your ideas in order.

Here are some ideas you may be able to include in your story web.

move to a new house	started school	learned a new sport
began scouts	music lessons	swimming lessons
made a new friend	learned a new skill	new teacher
new pet	a new addition to your family	special vacation
family activity	field trip	

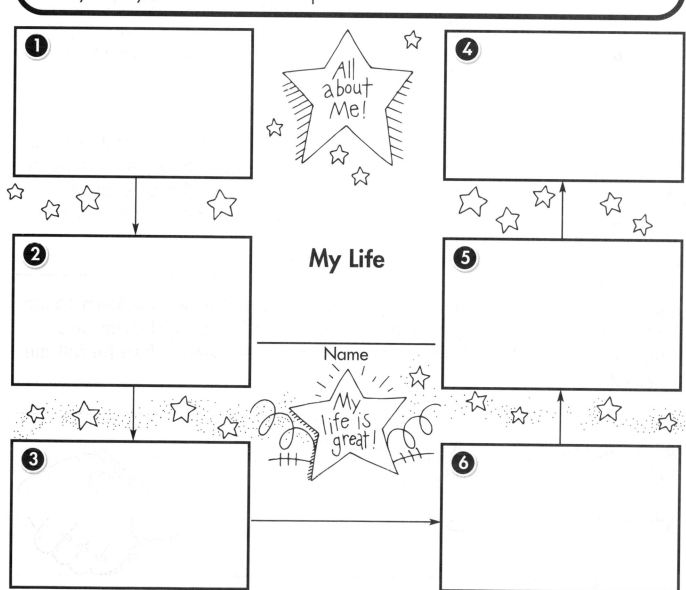

Traits of Good Writing • 2–3 © 2004 Creative Teaching Press

Name _____

Bye, Bye, Birdie

Analyzing Parts of a Story

Read the story. Answer the questions.

Sophie and Naomi were playing in the backyard when they found a bird in the tall grass. The bird couldn't fly. "Should we keep it?" Naomi asked. "Yes," declared Sophie. "We'll give it a good home until it can manage on its own."

The girls named the bird Peep. They filled a box with grass and sticks. They fed Peep birdseeds and gave him droplets of water from an eyedropper. Naomi even gave Peep flying lessons.

When the day came for the girls to let the bird go, Sophie placed Peep in her hands and lifted him high into the air. Peep flew away and the girls waved goodbye.

Then something funny happened. Peep began to fly back toward Sophie and Naomi. Carrying something in his beak, he came within five feet of the girls. Peep bent his wing toward the girls and dropped a piece of red ribbon onto the ground. "He just wanted to say goodbye," said Sophie, as she picked up the ribbon. Peep flew off again, never to return. "C'mon, let's cut the ribbon in half so we can each keep a piece," declared Sophie. "And then let's see what other animal we can find in the grass today," Naomi retorted. "YEAH!" exclaimed the girls in unison, as they looked at each other and smiled.

1 Who are the characters? _____

2 Where does the story take place? _____

3 What is the problem/conflict? _____

4 How does the story end, or how is the problem resolved? _____

_____

Traits of Good Writing • 2-3 © 2004 Creative Teaching Press

Attention Please!

Story Leads

The beginning of a story should get the reader's attention. Color the boxes with introductions that get your attention and make you want to read the rest of the story.

It was neat that the lollipop changed colors when you licked it. But I never thought I'd have a purple tongue when I went to the dentist.

How do you like a juicy foot-long, fresh off the grill? Ketchup and mustard? Pickles and onions? Mmmm. How about on a toasted bun with the works?

I was sitting by the lake, minding my own business, when a loud flapping noise nearly scared me half to death. It was a big old Mallard duck coming in for a landing.

Hot dogs are good. I eat them all the time.

I bit the lollipop. My tooth hurt real bad. I went to the dentist.

I was sitting by the lake. The duck landed in the water.

Write your own attention-getting introductions to replace this one.

The airplane took off. It flew up into the sky.

_____

_____

_____

All Is Well That Ends Well

Strong Endings

Read each pair of story endings. Color the box with the one that is more interesting and leaves you feeling satisfied.

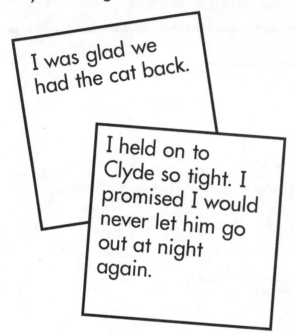

I was glad we had the cat back.

I held on to Clyde so tight. I promised I would never let him go out at night again.

It was a fun weekend at my grandma's.

Gosh, my grandma is so cool. I couldn't have planned a better weekend myself.

Write your own strong ending to replace this one.

We had a fun day at the beach.

_____

_____

_____

_____

Traits of Good Writing • 2–3 © 2004 Creative Teaching Press

One Fabulous Friday Night

Story Sequencing

Help complete the story web by filling in the missing details.

Introduction

I never would have imagined we could squeeze so much fun into one Friday night. My mom was right! She and Dad really know how to have a good time.

First

Then

Finally

Conclusion

By eleven o'clock I was so tired I almost dropped into bed. But it was worth it. That was definitely the most fun our family has had in a long, long time.

Crossword Fun

Parts of a Story

Complete the crossword puzzle with words from the word box.

conclusion   climax   conflict   characters   plot
setting   beginning   middle   end

Across

2. How the story ends
4. The most important moment or turning point of the story
5. The final part of the story
6. Where the story takes place

Down

1. The first part of the story
2. The people in the story
3. The center part of the story
4. The main problem in the story
7. The story line

Traits of Good Writing • 2–3 © 2004 Creative Teaching Press

Get Organized

Using a Graphic Organizer

Think of a story you want to write. Fill in the blanks of the graphic organizer to help you organize your thoughts.

Beginning

Here's how the story begins.

Who? Characters	Where? Setting	What? Conflict/Problem

Middle

Here's what happens next.

What happens?

Climax–most important moment

End

Here's how the story ends.

How does it end?   Conclusion

Name _____

What Is Voice?

Voice

Read the sentences about writing with voice. Use a word from the word box to complete each sentence.

| care | expression | feelings | unique | person |

1 Writing with voice shows you _____ about the message in your writing.

2 The author uses _____ to show feelings.

3 Writing with voice lets the reader know there's a _____ behind the words.

4 Writers have a _____ way of expressing themselves in their writing.

5 When writing with voice, authors share their _____ and emotions.

Draw a picture of a person who is feeling happy, sad, excited, or angry. Write what he or she has to say in the quotation bubble.

Traits of Good Writing • 2–3 © 2004 Creative Teaching Press

Name _____

Take Me Out to the Ball Game

Recognizing Voice

Read the sentences that describe a championship baseball game. Color the baseballs that contain sentences with a strong voice.

 We played baseball.

 Our team came from behind and won the championship game by two runs.

 We won the game.

 Everyone jumped up and cheered when Johnny struck out the last batter.

 Johnny is a good pitcher.

 It was a nice game.

 The fans went wild and so did I.

 There's nothing better than beating a tough team like the Tigers.

 Our team had fun.

 We were happy.

 It was the best game we ever played.

 It was a nice game.

 When I rounded third base, I knew we'd win the game.

Traits of Good Writing • 2–3 © 2004 Creative Teaching Press

Name _____

The Blizzard

Identifying Voice

A blizzard blew through Crandon, Wisconsin, dumping 11 inches of snow on the ground overnight. Different people in the community will respond differently to a blizzard. Read the comments from the five speakers. Look for the voice in each statement. Draw a line from each speaker to the matching text.

Parent

Child

Ski Resort Manager

Teacher

Snow Plow Driver

Yes! No school today! Look at that snow. This is the best day of my life. I'm getting up and going outside. Who's ready for a snowball fight?

I've been up since 4:00 this morning. Whew! This was a big one. I hope I'm at least halfway finished before rush hour traffic starts.

The hills are beautiful. Perfectly topped off with caps of white fluffy snow. There will probably be many skiers here today.

Oh, my! This is a lot of snow. I better arrange for a sitter. I have to get up and start shoveling or I'm never going to make it in on time.

This is wonderful. I could use a few extra hours of sleep. On the other hand, we have a lot to cover for that chapter test on Friday. I hope the kids will be ready to work extra hard tomorrow.

Traits of Good Writing • 2-3 © 2004 Creative Teaching Press

Sleepover

Identifying Voice

Read each statement. Circle the statements that have voice.

1. We slept at the zoo.

2. I'd never been to the zoo in the middle of the night before.

3. We walked in at night.

4. It was unusually quiet and especially dark that night.

5. I wonder what the reptiles thought of all of us kids sleeping in their building.

6. We brought sleeping bags.

7. Jamie and I curled up in our sleeping bags beneath the iguana display.

8. There were reptiles.

9. It was weird to hear the tortoises crawling around in the dark.

10. Cages of reptiles surrounded us.

11. We liked sleeping there.

12. It was the most exciting sleepover I've ever been to.

Name _____

Who's Talking?

Point of View

Point of view shows who is telling the story.
The **first person** point of view means that a character from the story is telling the story. The story will use the words **I**, **me**, and **we**.
The **third person** point of view means that someone outside the story is telling the story. This point of view will name the person or use the words **he**, **she**, or **they** in the story.

Read each sentence told from a third person point of view. Draw a line from each character in the story to show what he or she might say from the first person point of view.

The **third person** point of view

The **first person** point of view

| Naomi found a painted turtle that she wanted to keep for a pet. | Naomi | "I hope she's nice." |

| | Turtle | "Yeah! I've always wanted a turtle like this for a pet." |

| Joe was out walking his dog when it suddenly began to rain. | Rover | "Come on, Rover. We better get going." |

| | Joe | "I hope he can run faster than that." |

Now you try it. Read the sentence. Write two sentences in the spaces below that show a first person point of view.

| Jillian was so happy that she lifted her guinea pig high into the air. | What might Jillian say? | _____ _____ |
| | What might the guinea pig say? | _____ _____ |

Traits of Good Writing • 2–3 © 2004 Creative Teaching Press

Healthy Me

Cause and Effect

Cause-and-effect writing explains why certain things happen.
Example: If you eat candy for supper, lunch, and breakfast, you will not feel well.

Read each statement. Draw an arrow from each cause to its effect. Then write **cause** or **effect** to identify each statement.

I haven't been exercising at all.

I wasn't able to run very fast in gym class.

I don't brush and floss my teeth before going to bed.

I stayed up too late watching a movie.

I have two cavities. Yikes!

I'm dreadfully tired in school.

Mom made the best chocolate cake, and I ate three pieces.

I had the worst stomachache ever.

Write two cause-and-effect sentences of your own.

1 _____

_____

_____

2 _____

_____

_____

Traits of Good Writing • 2–3 © 2004 Creative Teaching Press

Name _____

Let's Talk About Pets

Dialogue

When people talk to each other, it is called **dialogue**. These two characters are talking about their pets.

Write the dialogue from the comic strip in the spaces below to show who's talking. Be sure to capitalize the first letter in each sentence of dialogue.

" _____,"said Latisha.

" _____!" said Jose. " _____."

" _____! _____?" Latisha asked, as she gathered the kitten into her arms.

" _____," declared Jose, as his pet snake, Stanley, gave him a great big hug.

If the snake could talk, what might it say?

" _____ "

 Draw a picture of you and a friend. Draw dialogue bubbles and write what you and your friend might say if you were discussing your favorite pets.

Traits of Good Writing · 2-3 © 2004 Creative Teaching Press

Persuade Me

Persuasive Writing

Persuasive writing is when you write to try to get others to do something, or believe your point of view. Persuasive writing requires voice. Without voice, the reader won't believe your viewpoint.

Draw a smiley face next to the statements with voice that will persuade the reader to believe the point of view.
Draw a sad face next to the statements that will not persuade the reader.

School should end at 1:00 p.m. each day.

1) _____ Families would have more time to spend together.

2) _____ Kids would have more time to do their homework.

3) _____ It's terrible that school is so long.

4) _____ Children would be more willing to do extra chores at home if they had more free time each day.

5) _____ We'd learn just as much playing computer games all afternoon.

6) _____ Teachers would appreciate having more time to correct papers and organize the classroom.

7) _____ My pencils always break.

8) _____ Children would be less rushed to get to piano lessons or soccer practice at 3:30.

9) _____ Kids would rather play laser tag.

10 _____ I'd rather be at the beach.

Describe It

Descriptive Words

Cross out the letters j, q, k ,v, and x inside the word puzzle. Circle each word as you find it in the puzzle. Print it beneath the heading it describes. Then write three of your own descriptive words for each heading.

```
q m e l t i n g v j k j q k v q x j q k v x q v
j k d r i z z l e q s w e e t v x c u t e k q x
k c r u n c h y v q x w e t j k c o l d k x k
j q f u r r y v f r u i t k j d r o p l e t s j x
j k q f r o z e n q j k j q v x a d o r a b l e
```

Apple

_____

_____

_____

Rain

_____

_____

_____

Ice Cream

_____

_____

_____

Hamster

_____

_____

_____

Traits of Good Writing • 2–3 © 2004 Creative Teaching Press

Name _____

Wonderful Words

Brainstorming Words

A good writer will use words that create a picture for the reader. The words should be descriptive, precise, and interesting. They should illustrate action and sound.

Read the words in the grid. Color in the boxes with words that are descriptive or interesting. Cross out the words that are not.

monstrous	splattered	went	treasure	prickly	put
seasick	go	avalanche	somersaults	got	clubhouse
looked	vanished	sunken	said	blustery	buzzed
adventure	hooted	sat	wobbled	squirmed	had
mysterious	will	galaxy	crash-landed	nice	shark
moved	pounced	crazy	stood	horrible	crunched

 Write three sentences using your favorite words from this page.

Traits of Good Writing • 2-3 © 2004 Creative Teaching Press

The Friendly Five

Descriptive Words

Using your five senses helps you think of descriptive words. Read the words on each snake. Color in the sections that contain describing words that match the sense on the snake's cap.

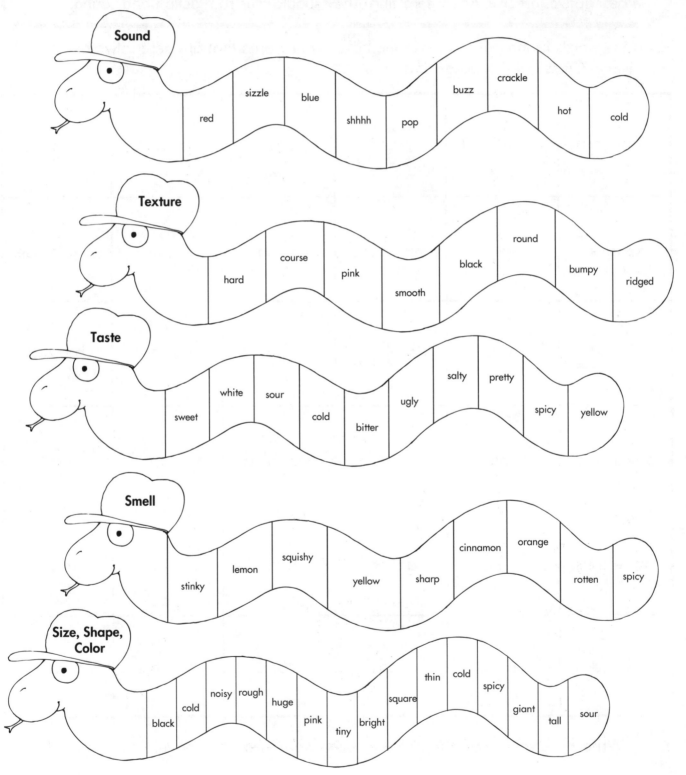

Traits of Good Writing • 2–3 © 2004 Creative Teaching Press

A Tasty Treat

Word Choice

Look at each pair of words. Circle the word in each pair that is more interesting than the other.

raining	frigid	hurled
drizzling	cold	threw
dreary	warm	eat
cloudy	cozy	gobble
talk	whispered	walked
chatter	said	marched
run	crept	toss
frolic	moved	put
shattered	went	yelled
broken	dashed	shrieked
saw	ate	ran
spied	devoured	pranced

 Put a star by the three words you like best. Make up sentences using these words.

Traits of Good Writing • 2-3 © 2004 Creative Teaching Press

Help the Reader See

Specific Nouns

Use specific nouns when you write to help create a mental picture for the reader. Read the noun on each pair of glasses. Choose a more specific noun from the word box and write it on the glasses.

hammer	poodle	kickball	skirt	breakfast
parrot	living room	chair	station wagon	

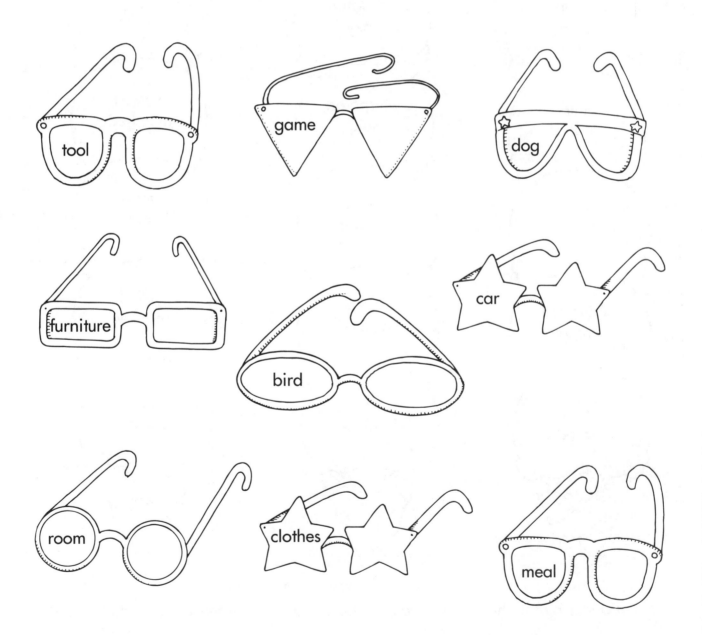

Traits of Good Writing • 2–3 © 2004 Creative Teaching Press

Name _____

A Better Word

Specific Verbs

Look at the underlined verb in each sentence. Find a specific verb from the word box to replace it. Write the new verb on the line. Reread each sentence with the new verb. The first one is done for you.

earn	skipped	glared	observed	shouted	whispered
won	build	determine	built	hike	adore

1. Dad will <u>see</u> which computer is best.   <u>determine</u>

2. Clarissa will <u>make</u> a dollhouse. _____

3. Stacie <u>went</u> to the park. _____

4. Bryce <u>looked</u> at me angrily. _____

5. We <u>got</u> a prize. _____

6. Rose <u>saw</u> the caterpillar. _____

7. Annie <u>said</u>, "I won!" _____

8. My dad <u>made</u> a new doghouse. _____

9. Lisa <u>told</u> the secret. _____

10. The boys will <u>go</u> along the trail. _____

11. We can <u>get</u> money by working hard. _____

12. I <u>like</u> my new puppy. _____

Name _____

Adding Adjectives

Adjectives

An **adjective** is a word that describes a noun. Adjectives help create a picture in the reader's mind. Adjectives make the writing more interesting.

Use two adjectives from the word box to complete each sentence and make it more interesting.

| pink | soft | fluffy | new | cuddly |
| black | old | red | shiny | white |

1. She wore _____ _____ slippers.

2. He rode his _____ _____ bicycle.

3. The _____ _____ barn was falling apart.

4. He had a _____ _____ pillow on his bed.

5. Mary picked the _____ _____ kitten for her pet.

Add two of your own adjectives to each sentence.

6. The _____ _____ dog pranced across the yard.

7. I landed a _____ _____ fish in the boat.

8. Walter watched the _____ _____ birds fly by.

9. Dad drove a _____ _____ car.

10. She chose to sit in the _____ _____ chair.

Traits of Good Writing • 2-3 © 2004 Creative Teaching Press

Name _____

My Bedroom

Descriptive Writing

Circle the words and phrases that tell about a third grader's bedroom.

dirty dishes
night-light
cozy
colorful
cement floor
all my things
quiet
peaceful
no roof
sunny
window
steering wheel
garbage dump
resting place
backseat

messy closet
my own place
sweep the garage
space to relax
frying chicken
comfortable
broken glass
headlights
dining room table
lots of pillows

puffy quilt
scary
soft carpet
shower stall
skateboarding
cold and windy
desk
baking a cake
dark at night
lawn mower

Write words and phrases that describe your bedroom.

_____

_____

_____

_____

_____

Traits of Good Writing • 2-3 © 2004 Creative Teaching Press

Antonym Match-Up

Antonyms

Antonyms are words that have opposite meanings.
Example: tall and short

Match each word with its antonym.

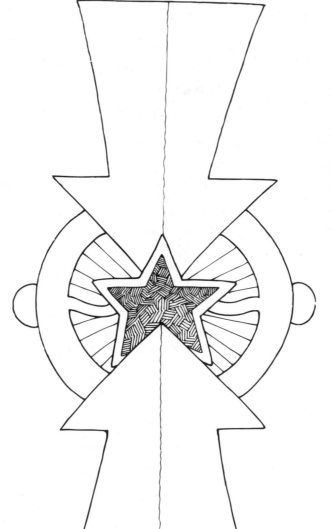

1) _____ high
2) _____ noisy
3) _____ exit
4) _____ shout
5) _____ best
6) _____ tight
7) _____ laugh
8) _____ fat
9) _____ weak
10) _____ accept
11) _____ dry
12) _____ rapid

a. enter
b. worst
c. thin
d. cry
e. strong
f. reject
g. low
h. slow
i. whisper
j. quiet
k. loose
l. wet

Traits of Good Writing • 2–3 © 2004 Creative Teaching Press

Sunflower Fun

Synonyms

Synonyms are words that have the same meaning. Example: small and little

Write the synonym for each word to complete the puzzle.

Across
2. jog
4. entire
5. jump
7. truthful
8. ocean
9. gleam

Down
1. enjoyable
2. genuine
3. peculiar
6. disappear
8. clever
10. orderly

fun   shine   sea
vanish smart   honest
run   odd   real
whole   leap   neat

Get Happy with Homonyms

Homonyms

Homonyms are words that sound the same but are spelled differently and have different meanings. It's important to know the correct spelling and meaning of a word when writing.

Read each sentence and the homonyms at the right. Write the correct word in each sentence.

1. It took one _____ to clean my bedroom.   hour   our

2. She bought new _____.   close   clothes

3. _____ like to go, too.   We'd   Weed

4. _____ cat is it?   Whose   Who's

5. May I ride _____ bike?   your   you're

6. I chose a matching _____ of socks.   pear   pair

7. _____ you like to ride along?   Wood   Would

8. She turned _____ years old.   ate   eight

9. He ran _____ the water.   through   threw

10. The _____ class enjoyed the game.   hole   whole

 Write a short story about a happy day in your life. Use some of the homonyms from above in your story.

Traits of Good Writing • 2–3 © 2004 Creative Teaching Press

Gum Balls Galore

Antonyms and Synonyms

Read the pair of words on each gum ball. If the words are antonyms, color the gum ball blue. If the words are synonyms, color the gum ball red.

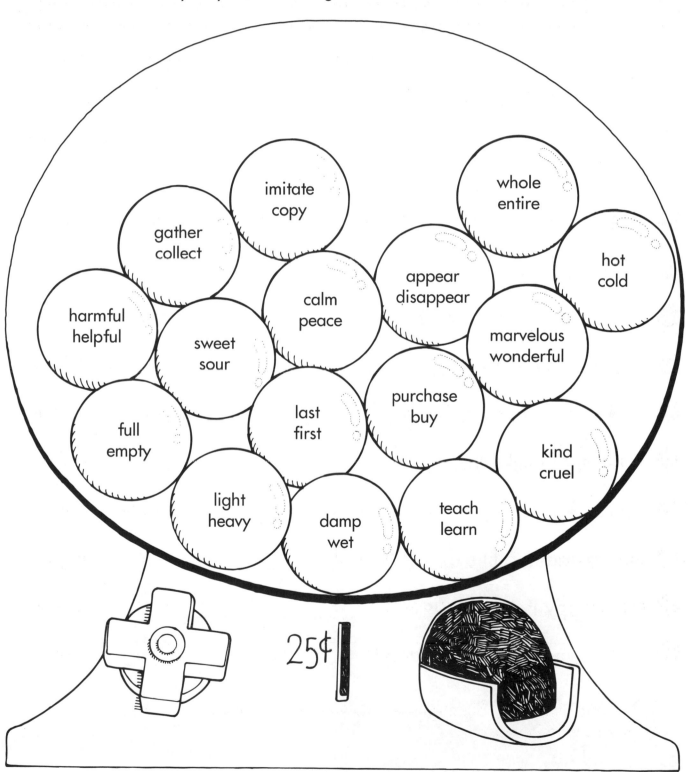

Name _____

Sam's Similes

Similes

A **simile** compares two things using the word *like* or *as*.

Sam is thinking of words he can use to complete the similes. Use a word from the word box to complete each simile.

turtle	night	snake	sun	wind	bird
house	bunny	bat	button	lion	snow

1 The ball was as slippery as a _____.

2 The room was as dark as _____.

3 Mary sings like a _____.

4 The man was as big as a _____.

5 It shined like the _____.

6 Her teeth were as white as _____.

7 The kite flew like the _____.

8 He roared like a _____.

9 Jimmy can hop like a _____.

10 Our puppy is as cute as a _____.

11 The old man was as blind as a _____.

12 She was as slow as a _____.

Traits of Good Writing • 2–3 © 2004 Creative Teaching Press

Write a Postcard

Word Choice

Read the two postcards. Which one is more interesting to read?

Dear Lydia,
    Florida is a nice state. You should come here someday. I'm having fun. It's sunny and warm.
        See you soon.
            Abby

Dear Lydia,
    You wouldn't believe what Florida is like! There are miles and miles of soft white sand, and tons of beautiful shells to collect. The Atlantic is crystal clear. I can stand in water up to my neck and still see my toes. It's exciting (and frightening) to ride on a surfboard and let the gigantic waves push you toward shore. We're gobbling up shrimp, oysters, and clams, morning, noon, and night. I'm having the best time of my life, but I miss you a lot.
            Abby

Write a postcard to a friend. Tell about your visit to a special place. Be sure to choose words that will make the postcard interesting and give the reader a clear picture of your experience.

Dear _____,

_____

_____

_____

_____

Name _____

Buy This!

Persuasive Writing

> **Persuasive writing** is when you write to try and get the reader to do something or believe your point of view.

Cross out the x's and circle the words in the puzzle below. Write them in the blank spaces of the ad to complete the sentences. Read the ad. Would it persuade you to buy the toy?

Ramrod Remote Control Car!

Hey Kids! Do you enjoy _____ remote control cars?
1

Then the Ramrod Remote is the perfect car for you. This car will

_____ and out perform any other remote control car on
2

the face of the _____ It's made from sturdy aluminum
3

that won't bend, dent, or _____ And it's wireless!
4

There are no long cords to get in your way while you play for

_____ on end. The car performs 360-degree flips and
5

_____, at the touch of your hand. Whether you like to
6

drive on smooth or rough terrain this car is _____.
7

Plus, this battery-operated vehicle is as _____ as a
8

mouse. Even your parents will love it. It's perfectly priced for the young

_____ at, only $9.99! Get one today while supplies last.
9

x	d	r	i	v	i	n	g	o	u	t	l	a	s	t	e	a	r	t	h	x
x	b	r	e	a	k	h	o	u	r	s	r	o	l	l	o	v	e	r	s	x
d	y	n	a	m	i	t	e	q	u	i	e	t	h	o	b	b	y	i	s	t

Write an ad for a toy you would like to sell.

Traits of Good Writing • 2–3 © 2004 Creative Teaching Press

Adventures in Alliteration

Alliteration

> **Alliteration** is a group of words that share the same beginning sound.
>   Examples:
>   Marsha munched marshmallows.
>   Paul put pickles in the pail.
>   Toby took a train to Tallahassee.

Make a list of words that begin with each letter. Be sure to include nouns and verbs.

C	B	T

Create sentences using the words you wrote. Include examples of alliteration for each letter.

C _____

_____

B _____

_____

T _____

_____

Name _____

Weak or Strong?

Topic Sentences

Read each pair of topic sentences. Color in the box with the topic sentence that uses words that grab your attention.

| I like going to the carnival. | Mom put supper on the table. |

| Ahhhh, there's nothing like the sights and sounds and smells of the carnival. | The crock of chili was piping hot, and the smell of the freshly baked bread made my mouth water. |

Now read the topic sentences below. Write new topic sentences that will grab the reader's attention. On another sheet of paper, draw a picture to match each new topic sentence.

I found a toad and picked it up.

_____

_____

_____

_____

It's fun to work in the garden.

_____

_____

_____

_____

Traits of Good Writing • 2–3 © 2004 Creative Teaching Press

Polly Helen Popplebee

Character Description

Read this character description.
Polly was 9 years old.
She wore a sweater and had two ponytails.
Polly thought she was very smart.

Now read this description of Polly.

Polly Helen Popplebee was nine and a half years old. "Almost ten," she would spout rather loudly if you asked her. Each day she tied her springy red hair into two ponytails at the top of her head. She wrapped each ponytail with three hair bands "to make them look bumpy like the humps on a camel," she declared to her closest friends. Some days Polly spent more than twenty minutes combing and tying her ponytails. She didn't mind. It was worth it to her. "The ponies are perfect," she'd say with a grin, and then pinch her own cheek for good luck.

Polly wore her favorite blue sweater almost every day. "It's a hand-me-down from my Great Aunt Alexis," she'd boast, even though the sweater was two sizes too big, and it hung on her like a tent.

Every morning when Polly got dressed, she would dig through her drawer for the brightest pair of striped knee socks she could find. Polly would carefully roll the socks down and around and around, so they would hug her ankles and sit like two big fat donuts on her feet. She said she wore her socks that way because she "liked to make a statement." Polly Helen Popplebee was convinced that she was the wisest girl in the town of Blooming Grove. And she let everyone know it!

Read the second description again. Circle the words that . . .

✓ make the character interesting
✓ add details about Polly
✓ help give you a picture of what Polly looks and acts like

Name _____

Who's Who?

Character Description

The way you describe a character should give the reader a clear picture of what the person looks or acts like. The reader should feel like he or she knows the character.

Read each character description. Write the name of the characters beneath their pictures.

a Dad was tired, hot, and breathing heavily. He wiped his brow with a handkerchief and smiled at me. "That was a hard run, son. But you know what? It felt great." Dad always has a good attitude and tries to do his best.

b She always wore colorful ribbons in her hair and bright-colored clothes. Chelsea spoke rather loudly and oftentimes too much; she was known as the school "chatterbox." Chelsea Chatterbox to be exact.

c I used to have a friend named Courtney Cramden, but now I think of her as Crabby Cramden. She doesn't have a kind word to say to anyone. She'll find something to complain about, no matter what.

d Aunt Tina always has a hug and a warm smile for me. Aunt Tina often invites me to stop over for a soda. When we sit on her front porch, she rocks in her rocking chair, sips her tea, and tells me stories of when she was younger.

_____ _____ _____ _____

Traits of Good Writing • 2–3 © 2004 Creative Teaching Press

Name _____

The Scariest Campout Ever!

Descriptive Words

Have you ever sat around a campfire and listened to a scary story? Circle the words that would be good to use in a story titled "The Scariest Campout Ever!" Then write four more scary words in the blank spaces.

suddenly   hot dog   nice   yell   darkness

_____   pitch-black   dark   bear

nervous   hambuger   screeching

shriek   frightened   bathtub   _____

panicked   flashlight   dangerous   puppy

tiptoed   _____   balloons   ice cream

noise   heard   tent   forest   afraid   loud

cotton candy   _____   scared

spooky   alarmed   terrified   behind

fearful   anxious   soda pop   fire

animal   monster   wondered   lantern

duckling   growled   shuddered   creaked

 Use some of the words you circled to write a scary story about an overnight campout. Be sure to include an exciting beginning and ending sentence. Draw an illustration to go along with your story.

Traits of Good Writing • 2-3 © 2004 Creative Teaching Press

Name _____

Gym Class

Correcting Run-ons and Fragments

Read the paragraph. Look for run-on sentences and fragments. Use a red pen to edit the text by adding or removing periods, commas, and capital letters where needed.

Gym class is my favorite class. In the school day. Mr. Austin is the best gym teacher he plays all the games with us. I won. The jump rope contest. I even beat Jeanne Kurth. When we played kickball. I ran the bases twice I scored two points. I caught. Two fly balls and made two outs. Everyone loves Battle Ball anyone can play it. Volleyball wasn't. My favorite game. Chloe was great. At scoring points. When I grow up. I think I'll be a gym teacher.

Traits of Good Writing • 2–3 © 2004 Creative Teaching Press

Moving Day

Verb Tense

Read the story. Find a word from the house to replace each word in bold. Cross out each word in bold and write the correct word above it.

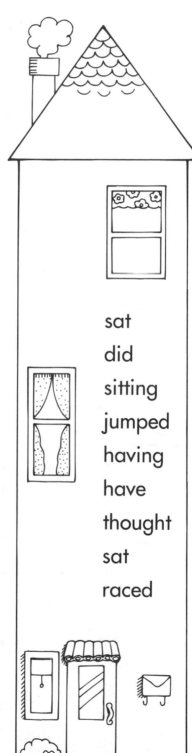

sat
did
sitting
jumped
having
have
thought
sat
raced

Charlie **sit** on the front porch of his new house. "I hope I **had** some friends in this neighborhood. I already miss my old friends," he **think** to himself. "I bet the gang is in the tree fort right now, **have** a great time."

"Why don't you go up to your new room, Charlie," his mother commented. "Maybe that will cheer you up." Charlie **does** as he was told. He **sit** on his bed for a while and then unpacked some of his toys. When he heard some noise in the backyard, he went to look out the window.

Charlie's heart **jumps** in his chest and a smile crossed his face. "I can't believe it!" he exclaimed. There was a big group of kids **sat** in his backyard. A "Welcome Charlie" sign and a huge bunch of balloons hung from the tree. "Maybe this won't be such a bad neighborhood after all," Charlie declared, as he **race** down the stairs, taking two steps at a time.

Traits of Good Writing • 2–3 © 2004 Creative Teaching Press

Name _____

Delightful Details

Adding Details

Adding details to sentences makes the sentences more interesting. Use the secret code to add words that tell where, when, why, or how about each subject and verb. Then add a period to each sentence.

① The horse trotted

_____
A ●

_____
B ■

_____
E ▲

_____
C ▲

② The woman waited

_____
B ●

_____
A ■

_____
B ▲

③ The dog played

_____
C ●

_____
B ■

_____
C ■

④ She showed up

_____
B ▬

_____
B ●

_____
C ▬

⑤ A friend called

_____
D ●

_____   _____
A ▲   D ■

⑥ The man ran

_____
D ▲

_____
E ■

_____
E ▬

_____
A ▬

	●	■	▲	▬
A	along	her	after	hill
B	for	the	husband	late
C	in	yard	path	supper
D	yesterday	school	up	south
E	winter	the	dusty	steep

Traits of Good Writing • 2-3 © 2004 Creative Teaching Press

Complete It

Complete Sentences

Draw a line from each subject to a predicate that makes sense. Then write more words after each predicate to make the sentence more interesting. Read your sentences aloud. The first one is done for you.

1 The store

2 Jennifer

3 Ken's bicycle

4 Jackson

5 My radio

6 Our cat

7 The zoo

8 My sister

is outside _____.

closes _____.

is singing _____.

opens at 10:00 a.m. on Sundays _____.

is hiding _____.

enjoys _____.

isn't working _____.

went swimming _____.

Name _____

At the Pond

Parts of a Sentence

> A complete sentence needs a subject, a predicate, a beginning capital letter, and an ending punctuation mark.

Use a red pen to complete these tasks:
- ❏ circle each subject
- ❏ underline each predicate
- ❏ capitalize each beginning letter, draw ≡ under the letter that should be capitalized
- ❏ add a punctuation mark at the end

1 (jason) <u>catches frogs</u>.

2 tanya picked up a turtle

3 did Jeanne pick up the litter

4 hallie found a caterpillar

5 they walked across the rocks

6 mom caught minnows

7 dad skipped stones

8 hudson found a fishing lure

9 she watched the geese

10 bryce scared the ducks

Traits of Good Writing • 2–3 © 2004 Creative Teaching Press

Too Much Water

Contractions

Using contractions will make your writing sound more natural, like someone is speaking. Cross out each pair of underlined words and write a contraction in its place. Color in the corresponding space on the bathtub for each contraction you use.

Dear Aunt Jaclyn and Uncle Dave,

I am writing to apologize for what happened on Saturday. I was not very proud of myself, and I know you were not very happy with me either. I did not mean for the bathtub to overflow. I was not trying to be irresponsible. I just turned on the water and did not think I would forget. I was having so much fun playing that I did not think twice about it. Then I remembered the water was on. I will not let that happen again. I was not thinking about what I was doing. I hope you are not mad at me. I am very sorry. Please do not forget that I love you.

Your niece,
Chelsea

| I'm | didn't | don't | weren't | didn't |
| I'm | wasn't | wasn't | wasn't | didn't |

Traits of Good Writing • 2–3 © 2004 Creative Teaching Press

Name _____

Long and Short Sentences

Varying Sentence Length

Using different lengths of sentences adds interest and rhythm to your writing. Read the two sets of descriptive sentences. Which one is more interesting?

The squirrel is cute.
It has a long tail.
Squirrels eat nuts.

or

The squirrel is a cute animal. It has a fluffy tail that's as long as its body. Squirrels eat nuts and seeds.

Read the sentences about dogs. Choose four sentences that you think would go well together and circle them. Be sure you choose sentences of different lengths. Then write them in the space below to make a paragraph.

- I like dogs.
- Dogs are fun.
- A dog makes a great pet.
- A dog can be your friend.
- Coming home to a dog is like getting a great big hug every day.

- Everyone should have a dog.
- Dogs are good.
- Dogs are nice.
- If you don't have a dog, you should get one soon.
- A dog is man's best friend.

_____

_____

_____

_____

_____

Traits of Good Writing • 2–3 © 2004 Creative Teaching Press

Name _____

Better Beginnings

Varying Sentence Beginnings

> To make your writing sound more natural, vary the way you begin your sentences.

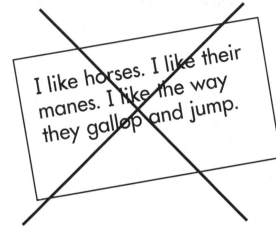

I like horses. I like their manes. I like the way they gallop and jump.

I like horses. Their manes are beautiful. It's exciting to watch them gallop and jump.

Rewrite the sentences. Be sure to vary the way each sentence begins.

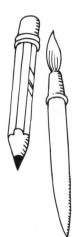

I like art class. I like drawings pictures. I like painting. I like to think of faraway places when I paint.

_____

_____

_____

_____

Bananas are yellow. Bananas smell good. Bananas taste delicious. Bananas have peels.

_____

_____

_____

_____

Traits of Good Writing • 2–3 © 2004 Creative Teaching Press

The Main Idea

Paragraph's Main Idea

Read the words in each box. Cross out the word that doesn't relate to the other words. Then unscramble each main idea and write it on the line. Draw a line from each box of words to the matching main idea.

puddles   candy bar umbrella boots   raincoat

1 grocery at store the

_____

tires   handlebars sandals spokes   helmet

2 the rain a walk in

_____

rolling pin   candle cutters sprinkles   dough

3 cookies make let's

_____

teapot   receipt cart groceries   money

4 awareness bicycle

_____

menu   television waitress silverware   napkin

5 restaurant favorite my

_____

Cross out the unrelated word in each box. Write a main idea for each word group.

birdseed   soil   plants garden   gloves   shovel

6 _____

chew stick cedar shavings food pellets feather duster water bottle

7 _____

Traits of Good Writing • 2–3 © 2004 Creative Teaching Press

Name _____

Two into One

Combining Sentences

Read each pair of sentences. Draw a line to the sentence on the right that combines the two sentences into one.

1 Ryan went to the store.
Ryan went to McDonald's.

2 Alana rode her bike to the park. Alana rode her bike to the school.

3 Brent has a new house.
Brent has a new swing set.

4 William picked up his lunch. William picked up his backpack.

Alana rode her bike to the park and then to school.

Brent has a new house and a new swing set.

William picked up his lunch and his backpack.

Ryan went to the store and then to McDonalds.

Now it's your turn. Combine each pair of sentences with the word "and."

5 Joe and Brandon ran at recess.
Joe and Brandon ran in gym class.

_____

_____

 6 Alexa found a kitten.
Alexa found a pair of keys.

_____

_____

Traits of Good Writing • 2-3 © 2004 Creative Teaching Press

Name _____

Spiders

Complex Sentences; Conjunctions

Use the conjunctions "and," "because," or "but" to join each pair of sentences. Color in each spider as you choose the word. Rewrite the new sentence. You might need to change, delete, or add a few other words so the sentence flows smoothly.

Example:
Spiders are creepy. Spiders are interesting to watch. (but because)
Spiders are creepy, but they are interesting to watch.

1 Spiders have eight legs. Spiders have two body parts.(because and)

_____

2 Spiders make great pets. Spiders sometimes scare people. (because but)

_____

3 Spiders are helpful. Spiders eat insects. (because but)

_____

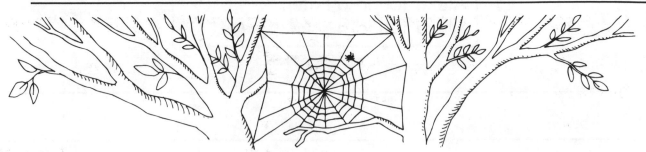

Traits of Good Writing • 2–3 © 2004 Creative Teaching Press

Birthday Fun

Conjunctions

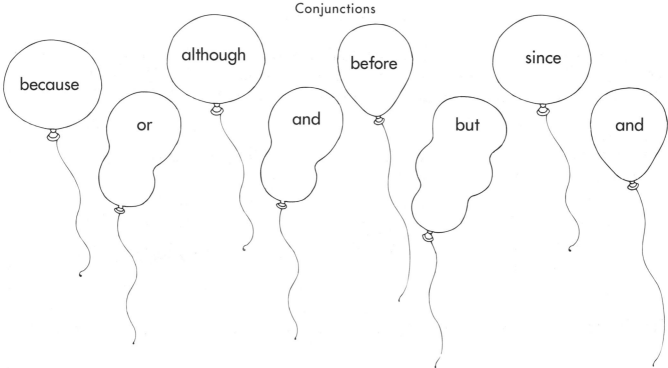

Read the conjunctions on the balloons. Read the sentences. Choose the conjunction that best completes each sentence and write it on the line. Color in each balloon as you use the word.

1 I can't wait for the party _____ my friends are coming.

2 We get to choose chocolate _____ vanilla ice cream.

3 Mom set out the noisemakers _____ the party hats.

4 I addressed the invitations _____ Mom mailed them.

5 We ate hot dogs _____ chips.

6 Melissa came, _____ she lives far away.

7 My puppy wanted cake, _____ we didn't give him any.

8 I can't believe it has been a year _____ my last birthday party.

Traits of Good Writing • 2–3 © 2004 Creative Teaching Press

Name _____

Recess and Pickles

Rhythm in Writing

Read the two descriptive paragraphs about recess. Count the words in each sentence and write the number at the end of the sentence. Which paragraph has more variety in length and structure?

A.

Recess is fun. ____
We play catch. ____
Jessie swings. ____
Joe runs fast. ____
The bell rings. ____
We line up fast. ____
It's time to go in. ____

B.

Nine fifteen is my favorite time of day.____ Recess time!____I love how all the kids run out the door, laughing, and smiling.____We all play different games and do different things.____Some kids play tag.____ Others like tether ball.____Usually some kids get together to play soccer.____Recess is the best.____Perhaps we should have recess all day long.____

Read the descriptive paragraph about pickles. Count the words in each sentence. Write the number words on the line.

Now rewrite the paragraph. Make it more interesting by adding words to some of the sentences. Write the number of words at the end of each sentence you write.

Pickles are good. ____
They're a great snack. ____
Pickles are green. ____
They are bumpy. ____
Everyone likes pickles. ____
Eat pickles for lunch. ____

Pickles

_____

_____

_____

_____

_____

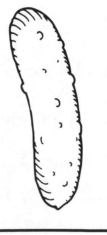

Traits of Good Writing • 2-3 © 2004 Creative Teaching Press

Camp Is Fun

Writing with Rhythm

Rewrite the letter. Use the checklist to help you make the letter more meaningful.

Checklist
✓ Vary sentence length.
✓ Vary sentence beginnings.
✓ Add details about camp.
✓ Add words to make the letter more interesting.

Dear Mom and Dad,
Camp is fun. I like it.
We do things. Camp
is great.
Love, Marcus

Dear Mom and Dad,

_____

_____

_____

_____

_____

_____

_____

_____

_____

_____

Traits of Good Writing • 2–3 © 2004 Creative Teaching Press

Name _____

Sledding

Removing Unnecessary Words

Read the story about sledding. The writer sometimes says the same thing twice. Cross out the words that aren't necessary.

Sledding is fun. Sledding is great. There's nothing better than sledding down a snow-covered hill on a cold winter December day. It's important to dress warm when you sled. Dress for the weather. You can ride down a hill alone or with a friend or by yourself.

Round saucer sleds are perfect for small hills. If you go down a big hill, you'll want a sled that you can steer. Round saucer sleds are better for small hills.

Our family sleds on Sunday afternoons. Mom brings hot chocolate and cookies. The cookies are always great. They taste good and yummy. One time my dad fell off the sled. He tumbled off the sled. Everyone laughed. He laughed. Sledding is the best fun winter sport. Hopefully it'll snow again soon.

Traits of Good Writing • 2-3 © 2004 Creative Teaching Press

Name _____

A Perfect Picnic

Expanding Sentences with Adjectives

Add adjectives to the sentences to make the writing more interesting and meaningful.

1. Jason ate a _____ sandwich.

2. We each had a _____ juice box.

3. Mrs. Kinsler made _____ brownies.

4. Jennifer brought _____ cookies.

5. It was a _____ spring day.

6. We sat on a _____ blanket.

7. Sarah poured _____ milk into

   _____ cups.

8. We sliced the _____ watermelon.

9. Even some _____ birds joined the fun.

Traits of Good Writing • 2-3 © 2004 Creative Teaching Press

Read All About It!

Capitalizing Book Titles

Capitalize all the main words in the title of a book.

Look at the five book titles. Rewrite each title using correct capitalization.

pippi longstocking

_____

Snow White and the Seven Dwarfs

the boxcar children

_____

james and the giant peach

_____

mr. popper's penguins

_____

lon po po

_____

Traits of Good Writing • 2–3 © 2004 Creative Teaching Press

Neighborhood Walk

Capitalization

Take a walk through this neighborhood. Travel only on the sidewalk squares that have names capitalized correctly. Color in these sidewalk squares.

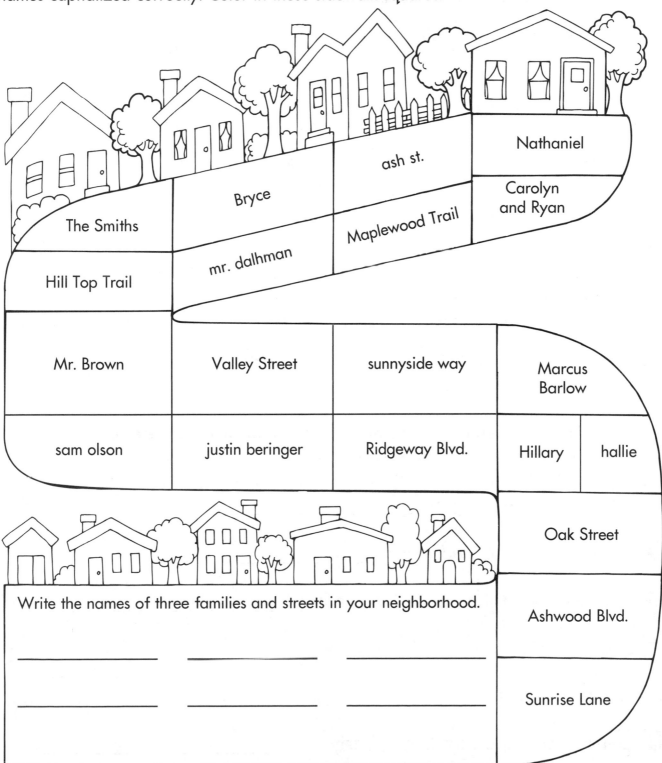

Nathaniel

ash st.

Carolyn and Ryan

Bryce

The Smiths

Maplewood Trail

mr. dalhman

Hill Top Trail

Mr. Brown

Valley Street

sunnyside way

Marcus Barlow

sam olson

justin beringer

Ridgeway Blvd.

Hillary

hallie

Oak Street

Write the names of three families and streets in your neighborhood.

_____ _____ _____

_____ _____ _____

Ashwood Blvd.

Sunrise Lane

Name _____

Travel Time

Capitalizing Cities and States

Liberty Island, New York

Seattle, Washington

Anchorage, Alaska

Aspen, Colorado

Honolulu, Hawaii

Orlando, Florida

Look at the U.S. map. Write the name of each city and state to complete each sentence. Be sure to capitalize the cities and states correctly.

1) Naomi went surfing in _____.

2) Joey rode a dog sled in _____.

3) Charles visited the Space Needle in _____.

4) Jessica picked oranges from a tree in _____.

5) Andrew went skiing in _____.

6) Geralyn saw the Statue of Liberty on _____.

Traits of Good Writing • 2-3 © 2004 Creative Teaching Press

Jordan's Schedule

Capitalization

Sunday	Monday	Tuesday	Wednesday	Thursday	Friday	Saturday
Zoo	Soccer Practice 6:00	Help Grandma after school!	Scouts	Piano 4:00 Homework pages 14,15	Finish volcano project	Scott and Kali come over

Answer the questions about Jordan's weekly calendar. Write each word in the space using correct capitalization.

1 What day does Jordan have soccer practice? _____

2 What day does Jordan go to the zoo? _____

3 What day does Jordan have Scouts? _____

4 What day does Jordan help his grandma? _____

5 What day do Jordan's cousins come over? _____

6 What day does Jordan plan to finish his science project?

_____

7 What day does Jordan have piano lessons? _____

Happy Holidays

Capitalization

What are your favorite holidays? Cross out the letters XQKZG on this page. Color in the boxes for the rest of the letters. Write each month and a holiday that occurs in that month inside the shape. Use correct capitalization.

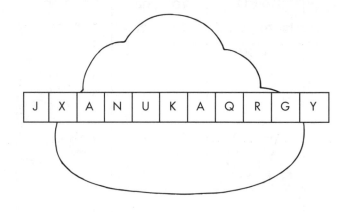

J X A N U K A Q R G Y

X F E Z B K R U Q A G R Y

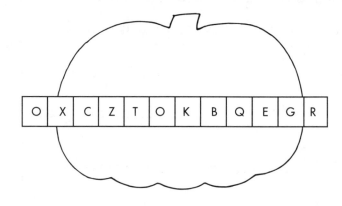

O X C Z T O K B Q E G R

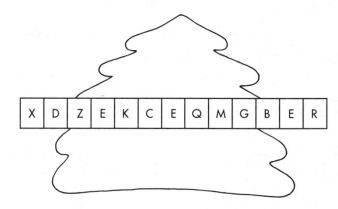

X D Z E K C E Q M G B E R

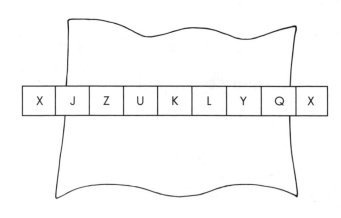

X J Z U K L Y Q X

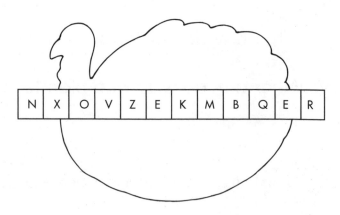

N X O V Z E K M B Q E R

Traits of Good Writing • 2-3 © 2004 Creative Teaching Press

Monthly Mix-Up

Capitalizing Months

Unscramble the letters to spell each month of the year. Write the 12 months in the correct order. Don't forget to capitalize each month.

_____

_____

_____

_____

_____

_____

_____

_____

_____

_____

_____

_____

ejun
onevebmr
erfrabyu
ylju
bdcemere
amy
ajunray
ortbcoe
ahrcm
rsetepbme
iarlp
guasut

Name _____

Tic-Tac-Toe

Capitalization and Punctuation

Color in all the boxes that contain titles that are punctuated and capitalized correctly. Try to get three in a row.

Ms Hallistead	Mr. Jameson	ms casperson
ms. schroeder	Mrs. O'Malley	dr. Jordan
ms parker	Ms. Danz	Mr. Schneider

Ms. springstead	mr. parman	Mr. Heathcote
Mr. burgess	Mrs. Mallow	Mrs. Denu
Dr. Michals	ms ryan	Dr Bauer

mr. Jones	Mr Pauley	MS Karls
Mrs. Masco	Ms. Brown	Dr. Green
Mrs. Severson	dr. Boyd	Mr. Kind

Ms. Tollefson	Mr. weber	dr. jarzemsky
mrs. Marx	Dr Van	Miss Porter
Mr. Bladow	Dr. Lower	Ms. Martinsen

Traits of Good Writing • 2-3 © 2004 Creative Teaching Press

Name _____

Curtain Call

Capitalization

This editing mark, $\underline{\underline{\ }}$ means you should capitalize the letter. Use this mark to edit the invitation.
Example: saturday
$\underline{\underline{\ }}$

Remember to capitalize:
- titles
- the beginning letter in a sentence
- proper nouns
- specific names of places and people
- words inside quotation marks

james and the giant peach

please come to our performance of james and the giant peach. The

play begins at 10 a.m. on monday, march 26th. we hope you can come.

we are asking people who attend our performance to make a one

dollar donation for the people in new guinea.

please call mrs. webster if you have any questions.

thank you!

mrs. webster's third grade class.

p.s. principal dahlman attended our dress rehearsal. he said "the

show was absolutely marvelous!"

cast: josh malone, serena wilkinson, jason brunner, mary traeger
stage crew: michael seston, jamal freeman, misty heathcote
director: mrs. webster

Traits of Good Writing • 2–3 © 2004 Creative Teaching Press

Name _____

It's in the Name

Capitalizing Proper Nouns

A **proper noun** gives the noun a specific name.

Read each noun. Write a proper noun to match it. Be sure to capitalize each proper noun you write.

cat

woman

girl

---

man

boy

dog

---

restaurant

street

store

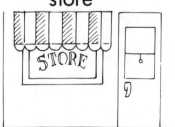

Traits of Good Writing • 2-3 © 2004 Creative Teaching Press

School Days

Punctuation

A statement ends with a period. A question ends with a question mark.

Write the correct form of punctuation at the end of each statement or question.

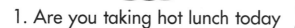
1. Are you taking hot lunch today

2. Sarah didn't finish her homework

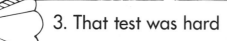
3. That test was hard

4. Sheila's locker wouldn't open

5. Would you like to play soccer at recess

6. Art class is my favorite time of day

7. What time is recess

Traits of Good Writing • 2–3 © 2004 Creative Teaching Press

Play Time

Sentences, Questions, and Punctuation

Rewrite each statement as a question. Rewrite each question as a statement.

Sentence:
I like to play four-square.

Question:
Do you like to play four-square?

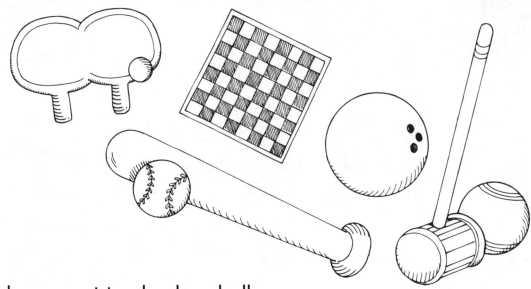

1 The boys want to play baseball.

_____

2 Can you play checkers?

_____

3 Do you like bowling?

_____

4 She is good at soccer.

_____

5 Are you good at Ping-Pong?

_____

6 Let's play croquet.

_____

Traits of Good Writing • 2–3 © 2004 Creative Teaching Press

Name _____

Soccer Team Talk

Exclamation Points and Question Marks

Add the correct punctuation mark by writing a question mark or an exclamation point in each dialogue bubble.

Traits of Good Writing • 2–3 © 2004 Creative Teaching Press

Don't Strike Out

Frequently Misspelled Words

Look at the misspelled words that are underlined in each sentence. Complete the crossword puzzle by spelling the words correctly.

Across

3. She called him <u>agin</u> because he did not hear the first time.
4. I like going to <u>scool</u>.
6. She is my best <u>frend</u>.
7. I like to <u>wach</u> cartoons.

Down

1. Once <u>apon</u> a time there was a princess
2. I wore two <u>diffrent</u> colored socks.
3. I <u>allways</u> eat my vegetables.
4. She <u>sayed</u> her mom is sick.
5. <u>Wen</u> are you coming home?

Traits of Good Writing • 2–3 © 2004 Creative Teaching Press

Shelly's Spelling List

Misspelled Words

Read the words. Some of the words are spelled correctly. Some of the words are misspelled. Rewrite the entire list of words on the blank spelling paper. Be sure to spell all the words correctly.

1 altho	**1**
2 likly	**2**
3 gramma	**3**
4 sometimes	**4**
5 hollidays	**5**
6 trying	**6**
7 insted	**7**
8 outsid	**8**
9 strate	**9**
10 wen	**10**

My Pen Pal

Misspelled Words

Read the letter Matthew wrote to his pen pal. Cross out each misspelled word and write the correct spelling above it.

Dear Chang,

How are you doin? I haven't heard from you in a long time.

I'm doin well. In scool we are learning about your cuntry,

China. I bet it's fun to live their. My family and I ate at a

Chinese resterunt last weekend. I thout about you. I had

chicken and rice. It was grate. I played soccer on Satirday.

We lost, but I had fun inyway.

I hop you rite back soon.

Sincerely,
Matthew

Traits of Good Writing • 2–3 © 2004 Creative Teaching Press

Climbing High

Parts of Speech; Parts of a Sentence

Read each definition, beginning at the bottom of the page with number 1. Circle the terms that match each definition as you climb up the tree.

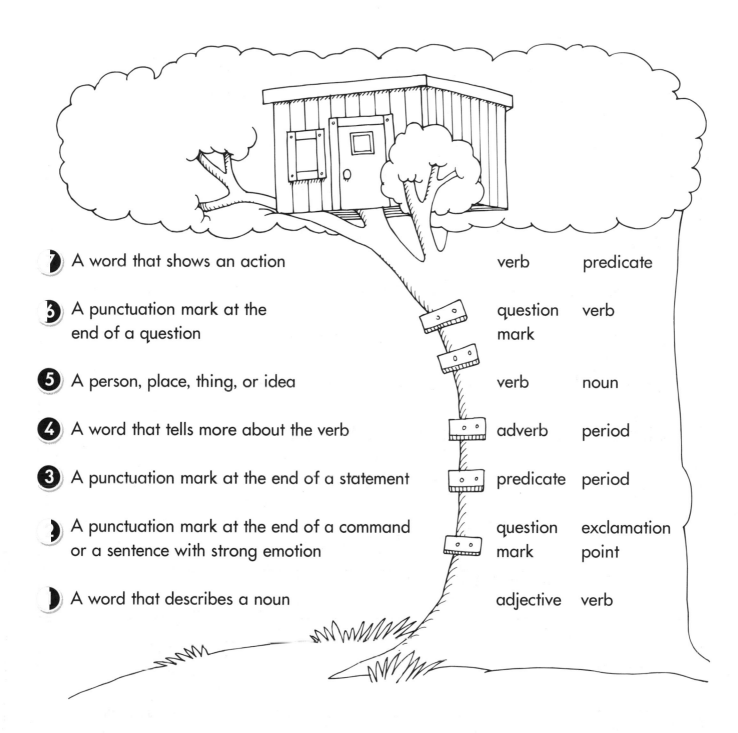

7 A word that shows an action	verb	predicate
6 A punctuation mark at the end of a question	question mark	verb
5 A person, place, thing, or idea	verb	noun
4 A word that tells more about the verb	adverb	period
3 A punctuation mark at the end of a statement	predicate	period
2 A punctuation mark at the end of a command or a sentence with strong emotion	question mark	exclamation point
1 A word that describes a noun	adjective	verb

Traits of Good Writing • 2–3 © 2004 Creative Teaching Press

Name _____

Spaghetti Is Best

Subjects and Predicates

Read each subject and predicate. Draw a line from each subject to the predicate that completes the sentence and makes the most sense. Choose four sentences to rewrite on the lines.

Subjects

Spaghetti

Parmesan cheese

My Mom

I

My little brother

The meatballs

Dad

Garlic bread

Predicates

is a tasty topping.

love spaghetti.

is my favorite meal.

makes spaghetti every Wednesday night.

wears a napkin as a bib.

goes great with spaghetti.

usually gets sauce on his shirt.

are the best part.

_____ _____

_____ _____

_____ _____

_____ _____

 Write two sentences about your favorite food. Be sure to include a subject and a predicate in each sentence.

Traits of Good Writing • 2–3 © 2004 Creative Teaching Press

At the Carnival

Subjects and Predicates

Look at the subjects in the word box. Choose a subject and then add your own predicate to make a complete sentence. Write four sentences on the lines. An example is shown below.

Dad	The carnival	Mom	The balloon	The soda
The clown	The ice cream	The ride	The cotton candy	

The clown is funny.

1 _____

2 _____

3 _____

4 _____

Traits of Good Writing • 2–3 © 2004 Creative Teaching Press

Name _____

Lunchtime

Complete Sentences

Read the sentences about lunchtime. Draw a diagonal line to separate the subject from the predicate.

Example: The milk/ is cold.
My fruit roll/ was chewy.

1 My juice box spilled.

2 I like tuna sandwiches.

3 I ate my chocolate cupcake.

4 Mom packed carrots and dip.

5 Strawberry yogurt is my favorite.

6 Crunchy chips are the best part of lunch.

7 Peanut butter sandwiches are always good.

8 The granola bar was apple flavored.

9 I stacked sliced cheese on small crackers.

Write two complete sentences about your favorite lunchtime foods. Draw a diagonal line in each sentence to separate the subject from the predicate.

_____

_____

_____

_____

Traits of Good Writing • 2–3 © 2004 Creative Teaching Press

Name _____

Bedroom Bonanza

Writing Commands

A **command** is a sentence that tells a person to do something. It begins with a capital letter and ends with a period. A command usually begins with an action word.

Examples: Clean your bedroom. Turn off the radio. Work quietly.

Rewrite each sentence as a command.

1 Will you please hang up your shirt?

_____

2 I would like you to clean your room.

_____

3 Your shirts need to be folded.

_____

4 Will you make your bed?

_____

5 I need you to put your toys away.

_____

6 Will you pick up all the things on the floor?

_____

Traits of Good Writing • 2–3 © 2004 Creative Teaching Press

A Day at the Farm

Nouns

A **noun** is a person, place, thing, or idea.

Read each sentence. Circle all the nouns.

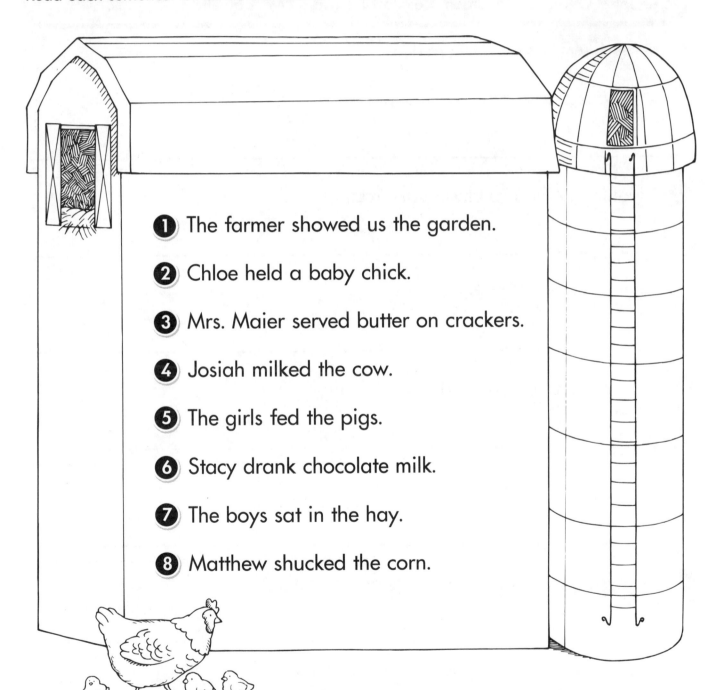

1. The farmer showed us the garden.

2. Chloe held a baby chick.

3. Mrs. Maier served butter on crackers.

4. Josiah milked the cow.

5. The girls fed the pigs.

6. Stacy drank chocolate milk.

7. The boys sat in the hay.

8. Matthew shucked the corn.

Traits of Good Writing • 2-3 © 2004 Creative Teaching Press

Pizza Party

Proper Nouns

A **proper noun** names a specific person, place, or thing.

Read each sentence. Write the proper noun on the line. The first one is done for you.

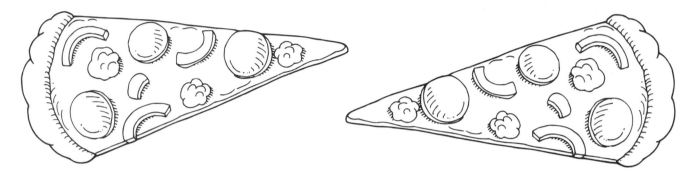

1 Mrs. Kalsow loves pepperoni pizza.   Mrs. Kalsow

2 We eat at Pizza Plaza a lot.   _____

3 Olives are Jordan's favorite toppings.   _____

4 My favorite restaurant is Pizza Pit Stop.   _____

5 My grandma ordered pizza from Charlie's Diner.   _____

6 Mr. Marx stopped for carryout pizza.   _____

7 The new pizza place will be on Maple Street.   _____

8 The girls walked to Pizza Palace.   _____

9 Isaac bought a frozen pizza from
Gander's Grocery.   _____

10 What's the name of your favorite
pizza place?   _____

Traits of Good Writing • 2-3 © 2004 Creative Teaching Press

Fun in the Forest

Pronouns

A **pronoun** takes the place of a noun.
Example: <u>Cathy</u> went to the forest. <u>She</u> went to the forest.

Underline the pronoun in each sentence. The first one is done for you.

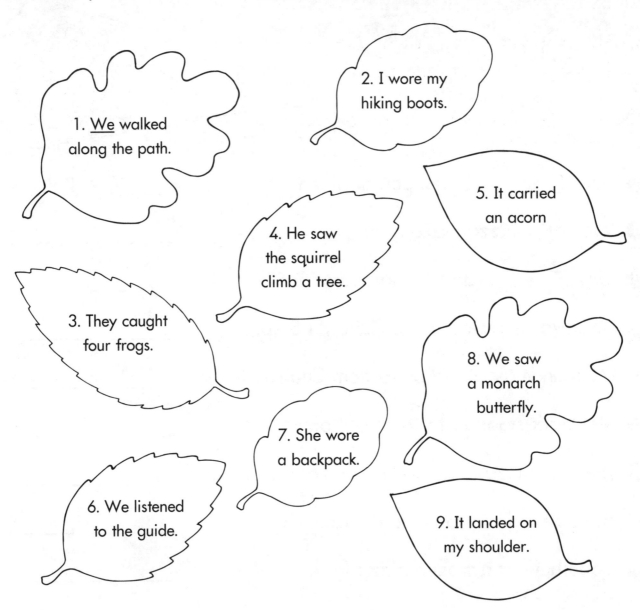

1. <u>We</u> walked along the path.

2. I wore my hiking boots.

3. They caught four frogs.

4. He saw the squirrel climb a tree.

5. It carried an acorn

6. We listened to the guide.

7. She wore a backpack.

8. We saw a monarch butterfly.

9. It landed on my shoulder.

Write a sentence about something fun in the forest. Use a pronoun in your sentence.

_____

Traits of Good Writing • 2–3 © 2004 Creative Teaching Press

Name _____

Aunt Betty

Common and Proper Nouns; Pronouns

Underline the common noun(s), proper noun(s), and pronoun in each sentence. Then write each noun only once in the chart below. Remember to start each proper noun with a capital letter. The first one is done for you.

1. <u>Aunt Betty</u> is a <u>nurse</u> at a <u>medical center</u>.

2. She is in charge of patients at the Lakefront Medical Center.

3. She has worked for the same doctor for five years.

4. She has a cat named Shadow.

5. Shadow likes to visit the dogs on Park Street.

6. Shadow eats fish every Monday.

7. Aunt Betty and Shadow play games together.

Common Nouns	Proper Nouns
nurse medical center	Aunt Betty

Traits of Good Writing • 2-3 © 2004 Creative Teaching Press

Name _____

Birthday Party

Singular and Plural Nouns

A noun that names only one person, place, or thing is called a **singular noun**.
A noun that names more than one person, place, or thing is called a **plural noun**.

Read about Sophie's birthday party. Look at the underlined nouns. Write each noun underneath the correct heading.

1 Sophie had a birthday <u>party</u>.

2 She invited seven <u>friends</u>.

3 Her mom baked a triple-decker, chocolate layer <u>cake</u>.

4 The children all brought <u>presents</u>.

5 We all put on party <u>hats</u>.

6 Everyone sang the birthday <u>song</u>.

7 The kids played in the tree <u>house</u>.

8 Sophie wrote seven thank-you <u>notes</u>.

Singular Nouns

Plural Nouns

Traits of Good Writing • 2–3 © 2004 Creative Teaching Press

Animals in Action

Verbs

A **verb** is a word that shows action or tells what the object or person does.

The verb in each sentence on this page is missing. Use a word from word box to complete each sentence. Draw each animal.

crawls	scurries	flies	slithers	plays
swims	hops	waddles	pounces	

The snake _____.	The caterpillar _____.	The panther _____.
His puppy _____.	My mouse _____.	Our fish _____.
Her bird _____.	The penguin _____.	The kangaroo _____.

 Make a list of animals you like. Write a sentence about each animal. Use a verb to describe each animal in action.

Traits of Good Writing • 2-3 © 2004 Creative Teaching Press

Name _____

Recess Time

Subject/Verb Agreement

Some verbs tell about what is happening now. Read the sentences about recess time.
Circle the verb tense that corresponds with the subject in each sentence.

1 Mrs. Ryan (blows/blow) the whistle.

2 Jeanne (jumps/jump) up.

3 Peter (plays/play) in the sand.

4 The boys (kick/kicks) the ball.

5 Hudson (climb/climbs) high.

6 Molly (runs/run) fast.

7 My friends (sit/sits) under the tree.

8 The girls (swings/swing) high.

Traits of Good Writing • 2–3 © 2004 Creative Teaching Press

Name _____

Dear Grandma

Past Tense Verbs

Read Nicki's letter to her grandma. Then help finish writing the letter by writing the past tense form of the verb in parentheses on each line.

Dear Grandma,

I'm sorry you _____ (miss) my soccer game. We beat the

Tigers six to three. I _____ (score) two goals. I

_____ (run) as fast as I could. I _____ (kick) the

ball a lot. I _____ (play) all four quarters. Mom and Dad

_____ (laugh) when I fell down. I _____ (rest)

during halftime. Boy, was I tired. Allie _____ (watch)

the game from her stroller. When the whistle _____ (blow)

at the end of the game, I _____ (jump) up and down.

Mom and Dad _____ (clap). I _____ (cheer) as

loudly as I could. The whole team _____ (play) a great

game. I hope you can come to my next game.

Love, Nicki

 Write a letter to someone you know. Tell them about a game you played or watched. Use several past tense verbs as you write.

Traits of Good Writing • 2–3 © 2004 Creative Teaching Press

Name _____

In the City

Run-on Sentences

When two or more sentences run together it is called a **run-on sentence**. Add punctuation and capital letters to correct the run-on sentences. Rewrite each sentence.

1) The stores are open early it's a busy day in the city.

_____

2) Many cars are stopped the people honk their horns.

_____

3) Lots of people cross the street it's a busy corner.

_____

4) It's noisy in the city the dogs bark loudly.

_____

5) The shoppers carry packages they are having fun.

_____

6) Two men walk into a restaurant they're going to eat lunch.

_____

7) A woman talks on her cell phone she's on her way home.

_____

8) Mr. James sweeps off the steps he puts a sign in the window.

_____

Traits of Good Writing • 2-3 © 2004 Creative Teaching Press

The Robot

Specific Verbs

Read each sentence. Replace the underlined verb with a more specific verb from the word box. Write each specific verb on the line.

gathered	created	discovered	constructed	ran
drew	admired	exclaimed	shouted	

1 I <u>saw</u> the idea in a magazine. _____

2 I <u>made</u> a robot. _____

3 First, I <u>got</u> lots of boxes and tubes. _____

4 Then, I <u>made</u> the arms and legs from cardboard tubes. _____

5 I <u>made</u> a face on its head. _____

6 I <u>said</u>, "This is fun." _____

7 I <u>went</u> to tell Mom about the robot. _____

8 Mom <u>saw</u> my project. _____

9 She <u>said</u>, "You did a great job!" _____

Traits of Good Writing • 2-3 © 2004 Creative Teaching Press

Name _____

A Cool Spelling Rule

Spelling

When a word ends with **e**, drop the **e** before adding "-ed" or "-ing".

Memorize this cool spelling rule, and then practice it. Write one new word by adding "-ed" or "-ing" to each base word.

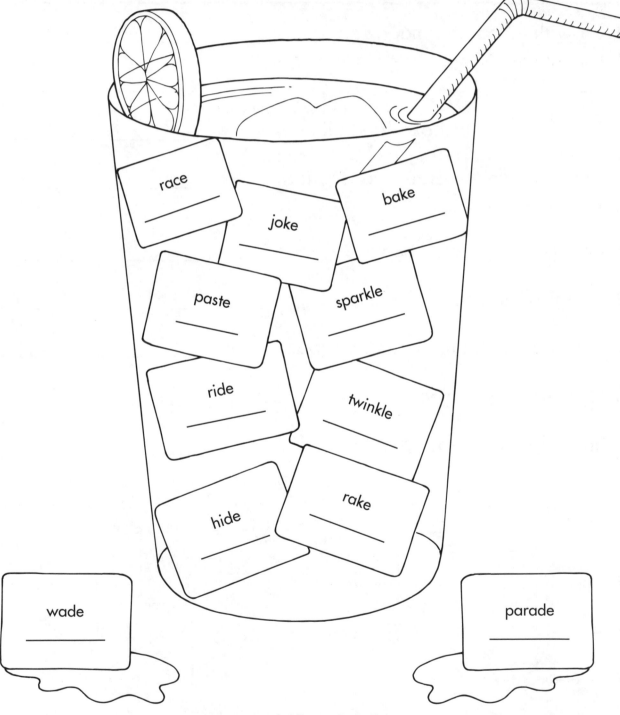

race _____

joke _____

bake _____

paste _____

sparkle _____

ride _____

twinkle _____

hide _____

rake _____

wade _____

parade _____

Traits of Good Writing • 2–3 © 2004 Creative Teaching Press

Name _____

Careful with Commas

Commas in a Series

Add commas as needed to each sentence. The first one is done for you.

1. Micah went to the zoo with Sophia, Zach, and Mrs. Gray.

2. Andy Drew and Joe came to play.

3. She juggles oranges apples and balls.

4. Oranges grow in California Florida and Texas.

5. Jackie wore a hat mittens and a scarf.

6. Mom served cereal toast and juice.

7. We ate hot dogs chips and pickles.

8. He collects rocks stamps and pencils.

Now write three sentences about some of the people in your family. In each sentence use a series of three or more words with commas.

9. _____

10. _____

11. _____

Traits of Good Writing • 2–3 © 2004 Creative Teaching Press

Name _____

Use the Right Word

Word Usage

Read each sentence. Circle the word that correctly completes the sentence.

1) My dog (is/are) playing.

2) The boys (is/are) singing.

3) The cats (is/are) sneaking through the yard.

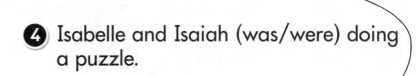

is

are

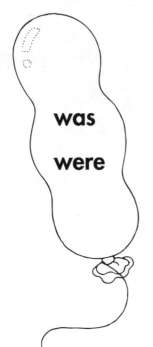

was

were

4) Isabelle and Isaiah (was/were) doing a puzzle.

5) Joshua (was/were) playing hide-and-seek.

6) The men (was/were) eating sandwiches.

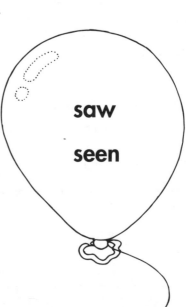

saw

seen

7) He (saw/seen) the movie yesterday.

8) I have not (saw/seen) her yet.

9) Ann (saw/seen) many animals at the zoo.

Traits of Good Writing • 2–3 © 2004 Creative Teaching Press

Just a Note

Word Usage

Rewrite each note using the correct word from the word box in place of each highlighted word.

gave	given	come	came	went
saw	seen	have	was	were

Dear Mom,

_____

_____

_____

_____

Dear Mom,
Mimi called to see if I could **came** over. I **gone** to her house.
Love, Sophie

Joe,

_____

_____

_____

_____

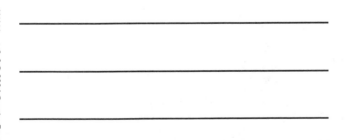

Joe,
Do you **has** the book I **given** you? I **come** over to borrow it, but you were gone.
Toby

Mr. Boston,

_____

_____

_____

_____

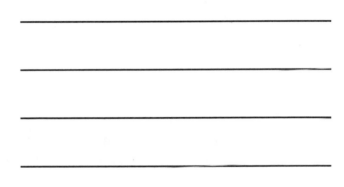

Mr. Boston,
Have you **saw** our mail? The postman may have **gave** it to you when we **was** gone.
The Murrays

What's the Buzz?

Using Quotation Marks

Quotation marks go around the words the person is saying.

Read each sentence. Add quotation marks to identify what each person says.

1. Marcie said, Look out for that beehive!

2. I hate bees, replied Jose

3. Lauren said, They won't bother you, if you don't bother them.

4. Mom smiled and whispered, I remember when two bees stung Dad.

5. Don't remind me! exclaimed Dad.

6. I think I'll stand over here, said Randy.

7. Me too, replied Jose.

Traits of Good Writing • 2–3 © 2004 Creative Teaching Press

Answer Key

What Do You Know? (page 5)

Answers will vary.

Picture Perfect (page 6)

Answers will vary.

Experiences (page 7)

Answers will vary. Possible answers include:

1. Washing My Dog
2. Working in the Garden
3. Fun in the Pool
4. A Day at the Beach
5. Life in the City
6. My Reading Marathon

Outdoor Fun (page 8)

Answers will vary.

It's Time to Write (page 9)

1. E
2. N
3. E
4. E
5. N
6. E
7. N
8. E
9. N

Let's Explore (page 10)

1. a
2. b
3. b
4. c
5. c
6. d

Project Pet (page 11)

Answers may vary slightly.

Daily Activities

eats

sleeps

plays

squeaks when I get home

Eats/Drinks

carrots

grass

water

oranges

apples

Fun Things to Do with Leah

build a maze for her

hold her

How to Care for Leah

bathe once a week

clean her cage

clip her nails

feed 2 times a day

brush her coat

My City (page 12)

Nature and Parks

Wisconsin River

Lake Marion

Indian Lake State Park

Crystal Lake

Restaurants

Lunch Bucket Café

Gordon's Diner

Taco City

Whistle Stop Sandwich Shop

Fun Places to Visit

The Cheese Factory

Historical Museum

Sky High Apple Orchard

Art Gallery

Annual Events and Activities
Annual City Garage Sale
July Fourth Celebration
Arts and Crafts Festival
Nature Days

Ideas and More (page 13)

Answers will vary.

A Humorous Story (page 14)

1. characters
2. setting
3. problem
4. first event
5. second event
6. third event
7. most important moment
8. conclusion

Details (page 15)

The second (longer) paragraph is more interesting and informative.
Details about the snowstorm will vary but should refer to a snowstorm.

A Trip to the Library (page 16)

The books that contain the following sentences should be colored:
The librarian said, "It's important to read a lot."
I found two books to help me with my report on iguanas.
Mom and I sat in the rockers and read.
Mom helped me find books I like.
The librarian helped us check out our books.

Start a Story (page 17)

Answers will vary.

For the Birds (page 18)

Answers will vary. Possible answers include:
1. They have long necks. They have feathers.
2. The ostrich lays eggs in the sand. The flamingo lays eggs in the mud. The ostrich grows to 8 feet tall. The flamingo grows to 5 feet tall.

A Friendly Letter (page 19)

Across
2. body
3. heading
4. signature

Down
1. closing
5. indent
6. greeting

Bake a Pizza (page 20)

1. Preheat the oven to 400 degrees.
2. Unwrap the pizza.
3. Place the pizza in the oven.
4. Bake it for 15 minutes.
5. Remove the pizza from the oven.
6. Cut into slices and enjoy.

Fishbowl (page 21)

Answers may vary. Possible answers include:
First
Second
Next
After that
Then
Finally

Make Your Bed (page 22)

2. Place the pillow at the top and center of the bed.
4. Pull up the blanket so that it covers the sheet.
6. Arrange your stuffed animals on top of the bed.

What's the Topic? (page 23)

1. The first sentence is circled.
   Topic–puppies
2. The first sentence is circled.
   Topic–fishing
3. The first sentence is circled.
   Topic–school
4. The first sentence is circled.
   Topic–grandpa

Cold Lunch Is Cool! (page 24)

The children who are saying the following sentences should be colored:

You don't have to wait in a long line to get your lunch.

You don't have to wonder about what's for lunch and worry that you might not like it.

You don't have to bring money to the office each week.

You can ask your mom to pack your favorite foods.

You can have a fun lunch box.

Kickball (page 25)

The balls next to the following sentences should be colored:

Stretch your legs before game time.

Wear good tennis shoes.

Practice running and kicking often.

Show good sportsmanship.

Cheer on your team.

Kick as hard as you can.

Be ready to catch a fly ball.

Concluding sentences will vary.

My Favorite Drinks (page 26)

Answers will vary. Possible answers include:
Orange juice is made from oranges. It is naturally sweet. It is good for you.

Basketball Days (page 27)

Answers will vary. Possible answers include:

1. Joe's basketball hoop was broken. He was sad.
2. Joe and his dad went to a store to buy a new hoop.
3. Joe's dad put the new basketball hoop together.
4. Joe and his friend were able to play basketball again.

Zachary's New Friends (page 28)

end

middle

beginning

My Life (page 29)

Answers will vary.

Bye, Bye, Birdie (page 30)

Sophie and Naomi
in the backyard
The bird can't fly. Should they keep it?
They let the bird go. The bird returns and says goodbye.

Attention Please! (page 31)

The boxes that contain these introductions should be colored in:

It was neat that the lollipop changed colors when you licked it. But I never thought I'd have a purple tongue when I went to the dentist.

How do you like a juicy foot-long, fresh off the grill? Ketchup and mustard? Pickles and onions? Mmmm. How about on a toasted bun with the works?

I was sitting by the lake, minding my own business, when a loud flapping noise nearly scared me to death. It was a big old Mallard duck coming in for a landing.

Writing will vary.

All Is Well That Ends Well (page 32)

The boxes that contain these introductions should be colored in:

I held on to Clyde so tight. I promised I would never let him go out at night again.

Gosh, my grandma is so cool. I couldn't have planned a better weekend myself.

Writing will vary.

One Fabulous Friday Night (page 33)

Answers will vary.

Crossword Fun (page 34)

Across

2. conclusion
4. climax
5. end
6. setting

Down

1. beginning
2. characters
3. middle
4. conflict
7. plot

Get Organized (page 35)

Answers will vary.

What Is Voice? (page 36)

1. care
2. expression
3. person
4. unique
5. feelings

Take Me Out to the Ball Game (page 37)

The baseballs next to these sentences should be colored in:

Our team came from behind and won the championship game by two runs.
Everyone jumped up and cheered when Johnny struck out the last batter.
The fans went wild and so did I.
There's nothing better than beating a tough team like the Tigers.
It was the best game we ever played.
When I rounded third base, I knew we'd win the game.

The Blizzard (page 38)

Parent—Oh, my! This is a lot of snow. I better arrange for a sitter. I have to get up and start shoveling or I'm never going to make it on time.
Child—Yes! No school today! Look at that snow. This is the best day of my life. I'm getting up and going outside. Who's ready for a snowball fight?
Ski Resort Manager—The hills are beautiful. Perfectly topped off with caps of white fluffy snow. There will probably be many skiers here today.
Teacher—This is wonderful. I could use a few extra hours of sleep. On the other hand, we have a lot to cover for that chapter test on Friday. I hope the kids will be ready to work extra hard tomorrow.
Snow Plow Driver—I've been up since 4:00 this morning. Whew! This was a big one. I hope I'm at least halfway finished before rush hour traffic starts.

Sleepover (page 39)

The following statements should be circled:

2. I'd never been to the zoo in the middle of the night before.
4. It was unusually quiet and especially dark that night.
5. I wonder what the reptiles thought of all of us kids sleeping in their building.
7. Jamie and I curled up in our sleeping bags beneath the iguana display.
9. It was weird to hear the tortoises crawling around in the dark.
12. It was the most exciting sleepover I've ever been to.

Who's Talking? (page 40)

1. Naomi—"Yeah! I've always wanted a turtle like this for a pet."
   Turtle—"I hope she's nice."
2. Rover—"I hope he can run faster than that."
   Joe—"Come on, Rover. We better get going."
3. Sentences will vary.

Healthy Me (page 41)

cause—I haven't been exercising at all.

effect—I wasn't able to run very fast in gym class.

cause—I don't brush and floss my teeth before going to bed.

effect—I have two cavities. Yikes!

cause—I stayed up too late watching a movie.

effect—I'm dreadfully tired in school.

cause—Mom made the best chocolate cake, and I ate three pieces.

effect—I had the worst stomachache ever.

Let's Talk About Pets (page 42)

"I think a kitten is the best pet ever," said Latisha.

"Not me!" said Jose. "I love snakes."

"Snakes! Why snakes?" Latisha asked, as she gathered the kitten into her arms.

"Because they love you back," declared Jose, as his pet snake, Stanley, gave him a great big hug.

Persuade Me (page 43)

The following sentences have a smiley face: 1,2,4,6,8.
The following sentences have a sad face: 3,5,7,9,10.

Describe It (page 44)

Apple—sweet, crunchy, fruit
Rain—drizzle, wet, droplets
Ice cream—melting, cold, frozen
Hamster—cute, furry, adorable

Wonderful Words (page 45)

The following words should be crossed out: went, put, go, got, looked, said, sat, had, will, nice, moved, stood. The boxes with the rest of the words should be colored in.

The Friendly Five (page 46)

Taste—sweet, sour, bitter, salty, spicy
Texture—hard, smooth, rough, bumpy, ridged
Smell—stinky, lemon, cinnamon, orange, rotten
Sound—sizzle, shhh, pop, buzz, crackle
Size, Shape, Color—black, huge, pink, tiny, bright, square, thin, giant, tall

A Tasty Treat (page 47)

The following words should be circled:
drizzling
dreary
chatter
frolic
shattered
spied
frigid
cozy
whispered
crept
dashed
devoured
hurled
gobble
marched
toss
shrieked
pranced

Help the Reader See (page 48)

tool/hammer	game/kickball
bird/parrot	dog/poodle
car/station wagon	room/living room
clothes/skirt	furniture/chair
meal/breakfast	

A Better Word (page 49)

1. determine
2. build
3. skipped
4. glared
5. won
6. observed
7. shouted
8. built
9. whispered
10. hike
11. earn
12. adore

Adding Adjectives (page 50)

1. pink fluffy
2. shiny new
3. old red
4. soft white
5. cuddly black
6–10. Answers will vary.

My Bedroom (page 51)

The following words and phrases should be circled: night-light, cozy, colorful, all my things, quiet, peaceful, sunny, window, resting place, messy closet, my own place, space to relax, comfortable, lots of pillows, puffy quilt, soft carpet, and desk.

Antonym Match-Up (page 52)

1. g
2. j
3. a
4. i
5. b
6. k
7. d
8. c
9. e
10. f
11. l
12. h

Sunflower Fun (page 53)

Across

2. run
4. whole
5. leap
7. honest
8. sea
9. shine

Down

1. fun
2. real
3. odd
6. vanish
8. smart
10. neat

Get Happy with Homonyms (page 54)

1. hour
2. clothes
3. We'd
4. Whose
5. your
6. pair
7. Would
8. eight
9. through
10. whole

Gum Balls Galore (page 55)

The gum balls with the following synonyms should be colored red:

gather/collect
imitate/copy
calm/peace
damp/wet
purchase/buy
whole/entire
marvelous/wonderful

The gum balls with the following antonyms should be colored blue:

harmful/helpful
full/empty
sweet/sour
light/heavy
last/first
appear/disappear
teach/learn
hot/cold
kind/cruel

Sam's Similes (page 56)

1. snake
2. night
3. bird
4. house
5. sun
6. snow
7. wind
8. lion
9. bunny
10. button
11. bat
12. turtle

Write a Postcard (page 57)

Answers will vary.

Buy This! (page 58)

1. driving
2. outlast
3. earth
4. break
5. hours
6. rollovers
7. dynamite
8. quiet
9. hobbyist

Adventures in Alliteration (page 59)

Answers will vary.

Weak or Strong? (page 60)

The boxes with the following sentences should be colored in:

Ahhhh, there's nothing like the sights and sounds and smells of the carnival.

The crock of chili was piping hot, and the smell of the freshly baked bread made my mouth water.

Writing will vary.

Polly Helen Popplebee (page 61)

Answers will vary.

Who's Who? (page 62)

1. d—Aunt Tina
2. c—Courtney
3. a—Dad
4. b—Chelsea

The Scariest Campout Ever! (page 63)

The following words should be circled: suddenly, pitch-black, dark, noise, heard, tent, forest, bear, screeching, shriek, yell, frightened, afraid, loud, scared, spooky, alarmed, panicked, terrified, nervous, behind, tiptoed, darkness, fearful, anxious, fire, animal, monster, wondered, flashlight, lantern, growled, shuddered. dangerous, and creaked.

Gym Class (page 64)

Gym class is my favorite class in the school day. Mr. Austin is the best gym teacher. He plays all the games with us.

I won the jump rope contest. I even beat Jeanne Kurth. When we played kickball, I ran the bases twice. I scored two points. I caught two fly balls and made two outs.

Everyone loves Battle Ball. Anyone can play it. Volleyball wasn't my favorite game. Chloe was great at scoring points. When I grow up, I think I'll be a gym teacher.

Moving Day (page 65)

The bold words should be replaced by these words:

sat
have
thought
having
did
sat
jumped
sitting
raced

Delightful Details (page 66)

1. along the dusty path.
2. for her husband.
3. in the yard.
4. late for supper.
5. yesterday after school.
6. up the steep hill.

Complete It (page 67)

Answers will vary.

At the Pond (page 68)

2. (tanya) picked up a turtle.
3. did (Jeanne) pick up the litter?
4. (hallie) found a caterpillar.
5. (they) walked across the rocks.
6. (mom) caught minnows.
7. (dad) skipped stones.
8. (hudson) found a fishing lure.
9. (she) watched the geese.
10. (bryce) scared the ducks.

Too Much Water (page 69)

The underlined words should be replaced with these contractions:

I'm
wasn't
weren't
didn't
wasn't
didn't
didn't
wasn't
I'm
don't

Long and Short Sentences (page 70)

Answers will vary. Possible answer includes: A dog makes a great pet. Coming home to a dog is like getting a great big hug every day. Everyone should have a dog. If you don't have a dog, you should get one soon.

Better Beginnings (page 71)

Answers will vary.

The Main Idea (page 72)

1. At the Grocery Store—receipt, cart, groceries, money
2. A Walk in the Rain—puddles, boots, umbrella, raincoat
3. Let's Make Cookies—rolling pin, sprinkles, cutters, dough
4. Bicycle Awareness—tires, handlebars, spokes, helmet
5. My Favorite Restaurant—menu, waitress, silverware, napkin
6. Main idea will vary. Cross out birdseed.
7. Main idea will vary. Cross out feather duster.

Two into One (page 73)

1. Ryan went to the store and then to McDonald's.
2. Alana rode her bike to the park and then to school.
3. Brent has a new house and a new swing set.
4. William picked up his lunch and his backpack.
5. Joe and Brandon ran at recess and in gym class.
6. Alexa found a kitten and a pair of keys.

Spiders (page 74)

Spiders have eight legs **and** two body parts.
Spiders make great pets, **but** they sometimes scare people.
Spiders are helpful **because** they eat insects.

Birthday Fun (page 75)

1. because
2. or
3. and
4. before
5. and
6. although
7. but
8. since

Recess and Pickles (page 76)

word count:
A. 3, 3, 2, 3, 3, 4, 5,
B. 8, 2, 13, 9, 4, 4, 8, 4, 8,
Pickles: 3, 4, 3, 3, 3, 4
Answers will vary.

Camp Is Fun (page 77)

Answers will vary.

Sledding (page 78)

The following sentences should be crossed out:
Sledding is great.
winter
Dress for the weather.
or by yourself
Round saucer sleds are better for small hills.
They taste good and yummy.
He tumbled off the sled.
He laughed.
fun

A Perfect Picnic (page 79)

Answers will vary.

Read All About It! (page 80)

Pippi Longstocking
The Boxcar Children
Mr. Popper's Penguins
James and the Giant Peach
Lon Po Po

Neighborhood Walk (page 81)

The squares with the following text should be colored in:
Nathaniel
Carolyn and Ryan
Maplewood Trail
Bryce
The Smiths
Hill Top Trail
Mr. Brown
Valley Street
Ridgeway Blvd.
Marcus Barlow
Hillary
Oak Street
Sunrise Lane
Ashwood Blvd.
Sunrise Lane

Travel Time (page 82)

1. Honolulu, Hawaii
2. Anchorage, Alaska
3. Seattle, Washington
4. Orlando, Florida
5. Aspen, Colorado
6. Liberty Island, New York

Jordan's Schedule (page 83)

1. Monday
2. Sunday
3. Wednesday
4. Tuesday
5. Saturday
6. Friday
7. Thursday

Happy Holidays (page 84)

January—New Years Day
February—Valentine's Day
October—Halloween
December—Christmas
July—Independence Day
November—Thanksgiving

Monthly Mix-Up (page 85)

	Correct Order
June	January
November	February
February	March
July	April
December	May
May	June
January	July
October	August
March	September
September	October
April	November
August	December

Tic-Tac-Toe (page 86)

Mr. Jameson Mrs. O'Malley Ms. Danz
Mr. Heathcote Mrs. Mallow Dr. Michals
Mrs. Masco Ms. Brown Dr. Green
Mr. Bladow Dr. Lower Ms. Martinsen

Curtain Call (page 87)

James and the giant peach
Please come to our performance of James and the giant
peach. The play begins at 10 a.m. on Monday,
March 26th. We hope you can come. We are asking
people who attend our performance to make a one
dollar donation for the people in New Guinea.
Please call Mrs. Webster if you have any questions.
Thank you!
Mrs. Webster's third grade class.
P.S. Principal Dahlman attended our dress rehearsal. He
said "The show was absolutely marvelous!"

Cast: Josh Malone, Serena Wilkinson, Jason Brunner,
Mary Traeger
Stage crew: Michael Seston, Jamal Freeman,
Misty Heathcote
Director: Mrs. Webster

It's in the Name (page 88)

Ansers will vary.

School Days (page 89)

1. ?
2. .
3. .
4. .
5. ?
6. .
7. ?

Play Time (page 90)

1. Do the boys want to play baseball?
2. You can play checkers.
3. I like bowling.
4. Is she good at soccer?
5. I'm good at Ping-Pong.
6. Do you want to play croquet?

Soccer Team Talk (page 91)

Did you see that kick?
What a great game!
Is the game over?
We won!
Did our soccer team score?
Can you be the goalie?
I love soccer!
Is it half time?
That was a great team effort!

Don't Strike Out (page 92)

Across
3. again
4. school
6. friend
7. watch

Down
1. upon
2. different
3. always
4. said
5. When

Shelly's Spelling List (page 93)

1. although
2. likely
3. grandma
4. sometimes
5. holidays
6. trying
7. instead
8. outside
9. straight
10. when

My Pen Pal (page 94)

The following words should be crossed out:
doing
doing
school
country
there
restaurant
thought
great
Saturday
anyway
hope
write

Climbing High (page 95)

7. verb
6. question mark
5. noun
4. adverb
3. period
2. exclamation point
1. adjective

Spaghetti Is Best (page 96)

Answers will vary.

At the Carnival (page 97)

Answers will vary.

Lunchtime (page 98)

1. My juice box /spilled.
2. I /like tuna sandwiches.
3. I /ate my chocolate cupcake.
4. Mom /packed carrots and dip.
5. Strawberry yogurt /is my favorite.
6. Crunchy chips /are the best part of lunch.
7. Peanut butter sandwiches /are always good.
8. The granola bar/ was apple flavored.
9. I /stacked sliced cheese on small crackers.

Bedroom Bonanza (page 99)

Answers will vary.

A Day at the Farm (page 100)

The following nouns should be circled:
1. farmer, garden
2. Chloe, chick
3. Mrs. Maier, butter, crackers
4. Joshua, cow
5. girls, pigs
6. Stacy, milk
7. boys, hay
8. Matthew, corn

Pizza Party (page 101)

2. Pizza Plaza
3. Jordan's
4. Pizza Pit Stop
5. Charlie's Diner
6. Mr. Marx
7. Maple Street
8. Pizza Palace
9. Gander's Grocery
10. Answers will vary.

Fun in the Forest (page 102)

The following words should be underlined:
1. We
2. I
3. They
4. He
5. It
6. We
7. She
8. We
9. It

Aunt Betty (page 103)

2. She is in charge of patients at the Lakefront Medical Center.
3. She has worked for the same doctor for five years.
4. She has a cat named Shadow.
5. Shadow likes to visit the dogs on Park Street.
6. Shadow eats fish every Monday.
7. Aunt Betty and Shadow play games together.

Common Nouns
nurse
medical center
patients
doctor
years
cat
dogs
day
fish
games

Proper Nouns
Aunt Betty
Lakefront Medical Center
Shadow
Park Street
Monday

Birthday Party (page 104)

Plural Nouns
friends
presents
hats
notes

Singular Nouns
party
cake
song
house

Animals in Action (page 105)

Answers may vary. Possible answers include:
The snake slithers.
The caterpillar crawls.
The panther pounces.
His puppy plays.
My mouse scurries.
Our fish swims.
Her bird flies.
The penguin waddles.
The kangaroo hops.

Recess Time (page 106)

1. blows
2. jumps
3. plays
4. kick
5. climbs
6. runs
7. sit
8. swing

Dear Grandma (page 107)

missed
scored
ran
kicked
played
laughed
rested
watched
blew
jumped
clapped
cheered
played

In the City (page 108)

Answers may vary. Possible answers include:
1. The stores are open early. It's a busy day in the city.
2. Many cars are stopped. The people honk their horns.
3. Lots of people cross the street. It's a busy corner.
4. It's noisy in the city. The dogs bark loudly.
5. The shoppers carry packages. They are having fun.
6. Two men walk into a restaurant. They're going to eat lunch.
7. A woman talks on her cell phone. She's on her way home.
8. Mr. James sweeps off the steps. He puts a sign in the window.

The Robot (page 109)

1. discovered
2. created
3. gathered
4. constructed
5. drew
6. shouted
7. ran
8. admired
9. exclaimed

A Cool Spelling Rule (page 110)

Answers will vary. Possible answers include:

raced/racing

joked/joking

baked/baking

pasted/pasting

sparkled/sparkling

riding

twinkled/twinkling

hiding

raked/raking

paraded/parading

waded/wading

Careful with Commas (page 111)

2. Andy, Drew, and Joe came to play.

3. She juggles oranges, apples, and balls.

4. Oranges grow in California, Florida, and Texas.

5. Jackie wore a hat, mittens, and a scarf.

6. Mom served cereal, toast, and juice.

7. We ate hot dogs, chips, and pickles.

8. He collects rocks, stamps, and pencils.

9—11. Sentences will vary.

Use the Right Word (page 112)

1. is

2. are

3. are

4. were

5. was

6. were

7. saw

8. seen

9. saw

Just a Note (page 113)

Dear Mom, Mimi called to see if I could **come** over. I **went** to her house. Love, Sophie

Joe, Do you **have** the book I **gave** you? I **came** over to borrow it, but you were gone. Toby

Mr. Boston, Have you **seen** our mail? The postman may have **given** it to you when we **were** gone. The Murrays

What's the Buzz? (page 114)

1. Marcie said, "Look out for that beehive!"

2. "I hate bees," replied Jose.

3. Lauren said, "They won't bother you, if you don't bother them."

4. Mom smiled and whispered, "I remember when two bees stung Dad."

5. "Don't remind me!" exclaimed Dad.

6. "I think I'll stand over here," said Randy.

7. "Me too," replied Jose.